delicious whispers full of details that would do a tabloid proud yet have no factual basis. Written in a friendly, conversational style, *Fractured Spirits* is an easy read that will enthrall and entertain, and - like all good ghost story collections - linger on in your mind long after you close the book and turn out the lights. After all, the stories are true."

**Ophelia Julien**, author of *Hunting Spirits, Saving Jake,* and *Haunted: A Bridgeton Park Cemetery Book*

# FRACTURED SPIRITS

*Hauntings at the Peoria State Hospital*

*by*

*Sylvia Shults*

www.darkcontinents.com

*Praise for Fractured Spiri*

"Brilliantly written, Sylvia
information to please any histo
tome. This fascinating read is th
read, offering detailed informat
and how ghost hunters perceiv
must-read if you're into stalkir
loaded with information. I hope
of the field, writes many more
all."

**Tamara Thorne**, author of *Et*
and contributor to *Encyclopedia of Haunted Places: Ghostly Locales From
Around the World*, compiled & edited by Jeff Belanger

"Sylvia Shults's *Fractured Spirits* is a fascinating, touching, creepy, riveting read -- a sort of Central Illinois Ghost Adventures -- set in the defunct chambers of the Peoria State Hospital. Shults is a natural story-teller, and she gets at something deeper and more poignant here than mere phantoms..."

**Jay Bonansinga**, New York Times bestselling co-author of *The
Walking Dead: The Road to Woodbury*

"And so Peoria State Hospital is haunted, rather like saying that Albert Einstein was a touch intelligent. Ms. Shults is not only a bona fide aficionado of the supernatural, she is a ghost hunter as well, and so her book is a feast of personal experiences, shared accounts of fellow investigators, and best of all, ghost stories . To her credit, she has also gone out of her way to debunk or lay bare many of the urban legends surrounding the place, the tales told in

# CONTENTS

# FOREWORD

*by Troy Taylor*

If ghosts are truly the personalities of those who once lived, can we assume that these spirits would reflect whatever turmoil and trouble plagued them in life? And if hauntings can sometimes be the effects of trauma that have imprinted themselves on the atmosphere of a place, then would a place where terror and insanity were commonplace be especially prone to these hauntings? As an answer to both of these questions, I would need point no further than to the strange events that have plagued the Peoria State Asylum in Bartonville, Illinois for the past few decades.

It is a place of macabre history and there are many tales to tell about this sad and forlorn place. They are strange stories of madness, of social reform, and yes, even of ghosts.

Prior to 1900, mental health care in Illinois barely existed. In those days, anyone suffering from a mental disorder was simply locked away from society in an asylum. These places offered no real chance for a cure because they were not places that were designed to treat the mentally ill. An asylum was actually a place where those so afflicted were warehoused and kept away from mainstream society in the same way that prisons were used to house criminals. Conditions were often extremely poor and treatment was not yet an option. Many asylums were barely fit for human habitation. They were filthy places of confinement where patients were often left in straitjackets, locked in restraints or even placed in cages if they were especially disturbed. Many of the inmates spent every day in shackles and chains.

Even the so-called "treatments" were barbaric. One of the favored treatments was what was called the "water cure," where a patient would be immersed naked in a tub of icy water and then taken to a tub of scalding water. It was believed that this might shock the system into sanity. And there was more horror. Female patients received a cold water douche, administered with a hose and then wet sheets were wrapped tightly around them to squeeze the blood vessels shut. This was followed by vigorous rubbing to restore circulation. These treatments were administered several times each week.

Not surprisingly, such techniques brought little success and most patients never improved. In the days before psychiatry and medication, most mental patients spent their entire lives locked up inside of an asylum. Things began to change around 1905, when new laws were passed and psychiatry began to promote the fact that the mentally ill could actually be helped, not just locked away and forgotten.

One man who was a leader in such social reform was Dr. George A. Zeller, who became the first superintendent of the Peoria asylum in 1898. He served in the Spanish-American War, worked as the Illinois State Alienist, then served the mental health field until his death in 1938. He is remembered today as one of the most influential mental health care providers in Illinois history.

The Peoria Asylum in Bartonville (named for the closest large town and railroad depot) opened under the leadership of Dr. Zeller and was totally different than any other asylum that had existed in Illinois. The hospital implemented what was called the "cottage system" and dozens of different buildings were used to house patients. There was also a dorm for the nursing staff, a store, a power house and a domestic building with a laundry, bakery and kitchen. Dr. Zeller also supervised the creation of cemeteries. Eventually, the burial grounds grew to include four different graveyards although the oldest cemetery would mark the location of the first ghost story to ever be associated with the hospital. And it was no mere folk tale, but a documented account of a supernatural event. The teller of the tale was Dr. George A. Zeller himself!

I have been writing about ghosts, hauntings, crime and the unexplained in Illinois for more than twenty years and while there are a number of places that I can say are truly haunted – there are few that have had the effect on me that the old asylum has had. There is no question that this is an eerie place and the history of the hospital is certainly interesting enough to justify the many reports that have been documented about it.

The reader must agree that the place certainly has the potential for a haunting. The atmosphere of the place alone is more than enough to justify the reports of apparitions and strange events that have been witnessed and documented within the walls of the remaining buildings. Years ago, I coined the phrase "residual hauntings" to describe locations where events have left an impression behind, like a recording of sights or sounds. For reasons that we don't yet understand, these impressions replay themselves, like a movie projector being turned on, and are seen and heard by unsuspecting witnesses. They aren't really ghosts, but memories of the past that have lingered behind. Such residual energies are often reported at old houses, on battlefields – and in hospitals and asylums.

There is also the matter of conscious and intelligent spirits that remain behind at various locations. These spirits – or personalities, if you will – stay behind because of some sort of unfinished business or because of confusion at the time of death that causes their energy to stay behind – perhaps like confusion caused because they were mentally ill. In addition, to many of the patients, the asylum was the only home that they ever really knew and perhaps when they died, they stayed behind at the place where they were most comfortable.

"The place is full of spirits" – it's something that I have heard said about the Peoria State Asylum on a number of occasions. In this case, I certainly think such a statement is true.

And just how full is it? You're going to find out in the pages ahead. Sylvia Shults has done a wonderful job of presenting both the history of the old asylum and the true tales of the hauntings that linger there. If you're easily frightened, I suggest reading this book with the lights on!

Happy Hauntings!
Troy Taylor
Founder, American Hauntings

*Dedicated to all of those who have spent time on the hilltop, especially those who have lingered past the asylum's closing.*

# INTRODUCTION

*"Isn't the human presence, the human touch, more humane, more efficacious than canvas and leather straps?"* -- *Dr. George A. Zeller*

Ghosts. Old hauntings. Secrets that refuse to die.

That's what I like in my fiction. Give me a nice thick chewy novel about buried secrets and abandoned buildings and hidden unspoken dread, and I am one happy reader. I love writing about the stuff, too. But in the book you're about to read, there's one important fact to remember, one that makes all the difference in the world.

The ghosts in this book are real.

I think it's safe to say that there is no other single place in central Illinois – not the Parkway Tavern on Farmington Road where the gangster Bernie Shelton was killed, not Springdale Cemetery, not even the Peoria Public Library – that has captured people's imagination like the Peoria State Hospital and its grounds. Stories of this place abound – stories of unspeakable cruelty, like the tale of the nurse who pushed a patient in a wheelchair down a flight of stairs, or the cook who was beaten to death by a deranged patient in the dining hall. Stories of responsibility, like Dr. George Zeller insisting on an eight-hour workday for his staff. Stories of tenderness, like Dr. Zeller repurposing the dreaded Utica cribs as mangers for the deer in the zoo, or Old Book weeping for the dead that he helped to bury. We imagine stories of the wearing grind of day-to-day life in a mental asylum – a place where the unwanted and unloved were forgotten, a place where people came to live a pallid existence of despair … or where they came to die.

There are other stories about this place too, tales that the history books will not reveal. These stories are told and retold every October with ghoulish relish. They are shared in schoolyards and around campfires. They are often told in a low tone, accompanied by a self-deprecating shrug and the disclaimer, "I don't really believe in ghosts, but I was walking past the Bowen Building one day, and I happened to look up at one of the windows…"

The story of the Peoria State Hospital is fascinating, complicated, sometimes heartbreaking, always enthralling. The cast of characters is worthy of a big-budget Hollywood movie. There is Dr. Zeller himself, and his dedicated staff. There are dozens of ghost seekers, from TAPS and other ghost hunting shows to high school kids looking for a thrill in the dark. There are serious paranormal investigators, and casual observers who just happened to be in the right place at the right time. And all the time, like a low, throbbing note just below the limits of human perception, there are the ghosts.

No one really knows why Bartonville, a smallish town right on the banks of the Illinois River just south of Peoria, is such a hotspot for the paranormal. But theories abound. Some say it's the fact that the Bowen Building was built out of limestone from the oldest quarry in the United States. The tailings from the construction of the building can still be seen, a hundred years later. There's lots of limestone in the area too; Bartonville's Limestone High School is a nod to this quirk of local geology. There is a theory among paranormal enthusiasts that limestone is a conductor of spiritual energy.

When the Peoria State Hospital closed in 1973, everything was left just as it was. Plates, clothes, bedding, patients' belongings, everything. People were reluctant to go into the buildings because of the lingering stigma of mental illness. The whole subject was so taboo that it kept out all but the most avid curiosity seekers for several years. So the place became a ghost town, left to its memories. There's a very plausible theory that the spirits were drawn to this place because it still seemed familiar to them. All their stuff was still there. The atmosphere was ripe for spirits to flock to a place they considered home – and that still looked and felt like the hospital they had known in life.

Centuries before the Peoria State Hospital was built, the land on which it stands may have been an Indian village. There is mention of this site on the records of Fort Creve Coeur, but it's unclear whether there was an actual village here, or if it was simply a burial mound.

So why is the Peoria State Hospital so incredibly haunted? The place is just crawling with ghosts. Is it the fact that it was built on top of a possible Native American burial mound? Is it because the artifacts of daily life drew the restless spirits back to a place they had called home? Is it because it was built from stone formed from the calcium in the skeletons of microscopic creatures, turning the buildings into conductors of psychic energy? Personally, I don't see why the answer can't be "all of the above". There's no scientific way to prove any of this, of course. We can't measure the psychic conductivity of limestone. But we can't measure love, either, and there's no doubt it exists.

I'll be privileged to be your guide as we explore the phenomena of the Peoria State Hospital. We'll meet Dr. Zeller, and I'll introduce you to dozens of people who have interacted with Zeller's legacy of caring. We'll talk with paranormal researchers. We'll listen to the stories of ordinary folks who have had experiences that were definitely out of the ordinary. And we'll meet the ghosts of the Peoria State Hospital.

Trust me, we will meet the ghosts.

Let's get one thing straight before we start. I know that some of you who pick up this book will be skeptics. You'll say, "Aw, I don't believe in ghosts." I want you to know that that attitude is perfectly fine by me. It won't hurt my feelings in the least. If that's you, no sweat. Enjoy the stories for what they are: just interesting stories. I hope I entertain you.

And for those of you who do believe, you guys are in for a *real* treat. This book is a collection of anecdotes that I've gathered over months and months of research. There's a bit of history to start off with, just to give you a feel for the events that resulted in this abandoned hospital becoming a hotbed of paranormal activity. Then we'll move on to the stories. I'm a paranormal investigator myself, so many of these stories are from my own visits to the asylum. I'm incredibly fortunate (and grateful!) to live within a ten-minute drive of one of the most haunted sites in the state.

When I first started out as a paranormal investigator, everything I knew about ghost hunting I learned from Scooby Doo. Poke around a haunted place until something weird happens, then shriek like a little girl and run in the opposite direction. (My research methods have gotten a bit more sophisticated over the years.)

But something really wonderful happened as I was collecting the stories that make up this book. The more I learned about the history of the Peoria State Hospital, and about the people who lived and worked there, the more I came to understand it. And just as with mental illness itself, it is understanding that lessens fear.

My first sight of the Peoria State Hospital was, of course, the brooding stone bulk of the Bowen Building. Later, I discovered Stone Country, the cemeteries, and the Pollak Hospital. Even though so many of the hospital buildings have been torn down – the cottages, the industrial building, which just fell to the wrecking ball a few years ago – I didn't realize that many of them still existed. During its years of operation, the Peoria State Hospital was its own insular little community. It produced its own food, including about a thousand loaves of bread a day to feed patients and employees. Patients sewed their own clothes and ran the laundry service for the entire place. Three farms supplied the hospital with fresh fruits, vegetables, milk, eggs, and meat. The asylum was a thriving place for decades, a place where tortured, ill people came to find acceptance, aid, and maybe even a little peace. Even now, years after the last nurse closed her file drawer and the last patient stumbled out, blinking, into the sunshine, the place still has a thriving afterlife. The influence of the asylum was so strong that decades after its closing, the spirits still consider it their home.

So many people have shared their stories with me. I realized very early on in writing this book that even after I typed "The End", the stories would still go on. I've tried my best to collect every interesting experience people were willing to share, but I know that these tales won't end with this book. People will continue to be fascinated with the spirits of the Peoria State Hospital. The Bowen Building, closed for several years because of the real threat of asbestos, opened back up to the public just before this book went to press. The wonderful Pollak Hospital, which I personally feel is more haunted even than the Bowen, is the site of an annual haunted house sponsored by the Junior Football League of Limestone High School in Bartonville. People will continue to have experiences. The stories will still go on.

As you read this book, you'll notice a little ghostie icon in the margins. This is your cue – lucky you! – that extra fun awaits you on the Internet. I've collected many EVPs and ghost photographs during the course of researching this book. Whenever you see the ghostie, that means that the EVP recording or photograph referenced in the text is available on the companion website to the book, www.facebook.com/FracturedSpirits. The Facebook fan page is also a forum for people to tell others about their own experiences at the Peoria State Hospital. Readers can visit the fan page, participate in conversations, and share their own stories, creating an interactive community dedicated to discussing the hauntings at the asylum.

I'd like you to keep something in mind while you're reading. I'm in quite a few of these stories. I was there for a lot of the investigations that I write about in these pages. But this book is not about me. It's a big, wide world out there, and there are quite a few more interesting things in it than me. Having said that, I've realized that my experiences in some of the stranger places of this world are what will open those places up for other people. I'll wander around a dark cemetery in the dead of night, to save you the trouble. I'll sit in a haunted morgue in the blackness, my only light the red glow of a digital voice recorder, so you don't have to. Think of me as your tour guide. I'll try my best to show you the most interesting sights and sounds that have popped up at the asylum over the years.

So join me for an exploration of one of the most haunted places in Illinois. Whether you believe in ghosts or not doesn't matter to me. I just want to show you around the place. It's a sunny, warm day, and you can see the sunlight sparkling on the river all the way from where we're standing, up on the bluff.

Let's take a walk, shall we?

# HISTORY

*"Note the dog that bounds at you when you enter the yard and frisks about you as you walk up the path, and then note the tethered dog tearing at his chain and threatening to tear you to pieces. It is the same with human beings, sane or otherwise."*

*Dr. George A. Zeller, October 19, 1906, in a paper presented in Springfield to the State Board of Charities.*

I started the research for this book as a paranormal investigator. I never intended to evolve into a historian, even though I do hold a master's degree in history. I had intended simply to tell the tales of the hauntings at the old asylum. But the deeper I dug, the more I realized that you can't investigate the hauntings at the Peoria State Hospital without knowing something about the history of the institution.

The story of the Peoria State Hospital has been told, and very well too, in two previous books. *Asylum Light* is a history of the hospital by James Sheridan Ward. *Bittersweet Memories* is a collection of reminiscences by doctors, nurses, staff, and former patients, gathered by Gary Lisman. These are mentioned in the Bibliography. I encourage my readers to explore these works; they are well written and informative, and they'll give a good sense of the asylum's background and the life of Dr. Zeller.

During my search for ghostly encounters, I heard a lot of stories about the history of the asylum and the treatment of its patients. Some of the stories just weren't true. There were a lot of convenient prejudices and useful fictions told about the hospital, stories told to justify the haunted reputation of the place.

Of course, if we're talking about haunted insane asylums, it's almost imperative that we mention lobotomies. The theory behind lobotomies is this: humans have the most developed frontal lobes in the animal kingdom. The frontal lobe of the human brain is the regulator of emotion and the seat of reason and planning. If the frontal lobe is malfunctioning, this can lead to anxiety, as well as the inability to make decisions (which increases the anxiety). Surgical disruption of the frontal lobe forces the brain to rewire itself, to form new neural pathways and more appropriate responses to emotions. The prefrontal lobotomy, the original procedure wherein the surgery was performed through the patient's temple, was invented in 1935 in Lisbon, Portugal by Egas Moniz, a psychiatrist, and Almeida Lima, a neurosurgeon. They found that it worked best on patients with a diagnosis of agitated depression.

A properly performed lobotomy had the potential to calm excited behavior. It may not have cured or even changed the underlying dementia, but it could change a manic, dangerous patient into a more stable individual. In extreme cases, it could turn a three-hundred-pound raving schizophrenic into the walking dead. This sounds barbaric to us. But Dr. Zeller was adamant in his insistence that women should be allowed to care for all of the patients on the hilltop, even the most dangerous ones. The philosophy at the Peoria State Hospital was one of non-restraint. The doctors during the 1940s used methods that today we would consider inhumane, including lobotomies and shock therapy. (Shock therapy was used to help schizophrenics and epileptics.) But it was all done with a dual purpose: both to calm the patients down so that their caregivers could interact with them, and to give the patients relief from their personal demons. The alternative was to strap them down and keep them in restraints for life. In giving women the freedom to serve the patients of the asylum, the doctors had to impose limits on the patients.

Dr. Zeller died in 1938. The first lobotomy performed on the hilltop was in 1939, and shock therapy began in 1940. In total, ninety-four lobotomies were performed at the asylum. These were mostly transorbital lobotomies, the so-called "icepick" procedure, where the doctor slid a sharp tool behind the eyeball and punched through the thin bone at the back of the eyesocket, and worked the tool up, then down, severing connections in the brain before withdrawing.

Dr. Walter J. Freeman, one of the biggest supporters of lobotomy and the inventor of the transorbital operation, never claimed that the procedure would cure mental illness. He always promoted lobotomy only as a last resort. Freeman also kept careful track of the results of the surgeries he did, and wrote follow-up reports for every case. Many patients were helped by the procedure, overcoming depression, and getting help with overcoming phobias and compulsive behavior. Even so, the side effects of lobotomy could be so gruesome that Freeman's own son admitted, "Talking about a successful lobotomy was like talking about a successful car accident."

Those patients who were released back to their families after a lobotomy had different reactions to the operation. Some of them suffered with inertia or convulsions, or regressed to childish behavior and incontinence. But others got profound relief from the operation, and were even able to return to their previous careers.

Freeman himself told a reporter that if transorbital lobotomy "enables the patient to sleep on a bed instead of under the bed, it is worthwhile."

Freeman nearly always performed lobotomies to treat illness, pain, or violent behavior. He never intended lobotomy as a tool for mind control. However, he did admit that lobotomizing patients often checked their violent outbursts, settled their emotions, and reduced damage to hospital property. Lobotomy did change patient behavior in ways that benefitted their caregivers, even if those changes weren't always good for the patient. At the Peoria State Hospital, an institution committed to non-restraint, the staff honestly felt that this was the best alternative to shackles and straitjackets.

During the early part of the twentieth century, the mentally ill were often confined to institutions. The first few decades of the century saw a leap forward in research into mental illness. Psychiatrists were hard at work describing and classifying mental disorders. At the same time, asylums were seeing a huge increase in admissions. During most of the nineteenth century, the mentally ill were cared for by their families, or confined in poorhouses. But by the time Dr. Zeller took over in Bartonville, institution of psychiatric cases had become commonplace. Between 1903 and 1933, psychiatric hospitals more than doubled in size, some housing more than ten thousand patients. Unfortunately, up until the discovery of psychotropic drugs in the 1960s, there was little that hospitals could do for mentally ill patients beyond providing them with food, clothing and shelter until they got better on their own. This did happen sometimes.

In the state hospitals, patients tended to receive more personalized care than outpatients do today – by which I mean that their caretakers saw them on a daily basis, and were able to follow their progress much more closely. This gave doctors and nurses the chance to record rich personal details about the patients under their care. Sometimes, these glimpses into the lives of the mentally ill manage to be charming and horrifying at the same time. A record from a psychiatric facility in

Washington DC describes a female patient who, over the course of a couple of weeks, ate all of the straw off of a broom. There are several head-scratching entries in the Logan County Insane and Conservator's Record. This document covers the years 1856 to 1963, and is a record of committals for the insane of Logan County, Illinois. These people, after the court hearings to determine their insanity, became inmates of the Jacksonville State Hospital, the Illinois Eastern Hospital for the Insane in Kankakee, and the Peoria State Hospital.

The reasons for committal sometimes seem to be, well, petty. Of course there are several committals for menopause, "nonappearance of the mensis", and masturbation, including one early case where a patient was said to have developed "epilepsy growing out of onanism" (1883). There are several early committals for sunstroke or for overheating. One of these cases, a committal for sunstroke, led to the patient being declared insane for 25 years (1890). One of the heat stroke victims was declared to be "suffering from cerebral softening" (1909).

The records from 1905 to 1921 contain valuable descriptions of the patients' behavior. A suicidal patient "has threatened that if he could get a knife, he would end it all". A depressed patient is described as "refusing to eat, desiring to die, destructive of clothing, indifferent as to personal appearance". Some other unusual cases include a committal for fright from thunderstorm (1860), one for disappointment in marriage (before 1884), and another for "mental derangements and a gunshot wound of the brain" (1907). One record is particularly poignant. A mother "fears that she will do herself or [her children] harm ... feels that neither she nor they are right".

All of these oddities argue for the asylum as a place of refuge, a place where people who were truly suffering could go to be with others who understood their maladies. So many of the entries in the Logan County record reflect this: patients are "suffering from mental instability", "addicted to the excessive use of alcoholic liquors", "afflicted with mental delusions". It was also a place where they could find useful occupation. Yes, the patients provided a source of cheap labor for the hospital. The Peoria State Hospital, like many other institutions, was a self-supporting community. But rather than simple drudgery, work was seen as a form of therapy for the inmates of the asylum.

The community and companionship that work provided was vital for the patients, who might otherwise be isolated in their own mental worlds. Work, and the company of others, provided a distraction from their own psychoses and hallucinations. An obsessive could gently be led to another outlet for his energy. A patient who was too manic or disturbed to interact with her fellow humans could retreat into the quiet solace of caring for plants or animals. The work these patients performed also gave them opportunities to learn and practice life skills in a safe, nonthreatening setting – something that their mental illness might not have allowed outside the asylum.

Before the 1940s, there was a thriving occupational therapy program at the asylum. Everything on the hilltop was manufactured by the patients. The program was shut down in 1940, two years after Dr. Zeller's death. There was an uptick in patient violence after that, and the occupational therapy program was reinstated in the 1960s, with more of an emphasis on arts and crafts, rather than the work therapy of previous years.

In the 1960s, though, state labor laws changed, and by the 1970s patients were no longer allowed to work. This was done, sadly, with the best of intentions. The legislators wanted to avoid any labor abuses of the patients. However, these laws were based on legal interpretations of patients' rights, but paid little attention to their needs. It was just not as fulfilling for them to fritter away their time on arts and crafts as it was to do useful labor. These new laws restricting work ultimately did as much damage to the patients as they did to the hospitals, which fell into neglected decay. Without a reason to get up in the mornings, patients were reduced to aimlessly wandering the halls, or worse, sitting catatonic in front of televisions. Their minds and bodies were no longer kept active, and they began to suffer because of it.

Lots of new drugs also came out of research done between the 1960s and 1980s. At first, they were hailed as miracle cures. Chlorpromazine, marketed under the brand name Thorazine (for the Norse god Thor), gained FDA approval in March 1954. It was welcomed as a "chemical lobotomy", giving relief to schizophrenics by calming their frontal lobe misfirings without the invasive horror of a prefrontal or transorbital lobotomy. It was also cheaper. But soon, doctors and patients alike discovered that some of the side effects of these new drugs were worse than the psychoses they were designed to treat. Let's face it, anything that jolts your brain enough to jar a mania loose is going to have side effects.

Neuroleptic drugs, like lithium, amitriptyline, and diazepam, were administered in an effort to keep the brain calm enough to straighten itself out. But the side effects could be catastrophic. Tardive dyskinesia (TD) was first documented in 1973, although the condition had been noticed as early as 1958. A patient with TD suffers from facial grimaces and random twitching of the hands and arms. The condition is irreversible. Doctors realized early on that neuroleptic drugs produced Parkinson's-like symptoms, TD being the worst. But rather than admit that the drugs were causing neurological damage, they chose to interpret patients' uncontrollable twitching as a sign that the drugs were working. In addition to tardive dyskinesia, some neuroleptic drugs can have other serious side effects like weight gain and diabetes.

Even the short term effects of Thorazine are fairly horrifying: drowsiness, thirst, blurry vision, weight gain, tremors, and stiffness in the muscles of the arms and legs (causing the patient to clomp around in the "Thorazine Shuffle"). Thorazine works by blocking dopamine receptors. Dopamine is a part of what causes delusions and hallucinations. So, Thorazine diminishes those symptoms of psychosis. But dopamine is also part of what causes our brains to feel pleasure. So anything that blocks it deadens spontaneity and joy, and throws a leaden blanket over any source of pleasure. Someone on Thorazine can just sit in a motionless stupor for hours. "The chemical lobotomy" is, sadly, a horribly accurate description of the effects of the drug.

With the widespread use of these drugs, treatment methods moved towards an outpatient system, rather than constant, live-in supervision. Patients were brought to a hospital by family, given the drugs, then released back to their family's care within weeks or even days of admission. Some patients, when they encountered side effects such as lowered energy, apathy, lack of motivation, or muscle spasms, simply stopped taking the drugs. Without a system of support and supervision, many patients had to be readmitted later.

In the 1960s, the Bowen Building was remodeled, turning it from the nurses' school into an administration building. In 1964, the employees' dining hall was badly damaged by fire. The hospital decided not to rebuild it.

The mid-1960s remodel turned out to be the downfall of the Peoria State Hospital. The asylum asked the state of Illinois for funds to pay for the work. An investigation found that the Peoria State Hospital was the most successful hospital in the country for curing patients and reintegrating them into society. Unfortunately, the study also found that the asylum was also the most expensive. The state wanted to close the asylum. Instead of shuttering the place outright, though, legislators took the easy way out, hoping perhaps that the hospital would fail on its own. The cottage system, the semblance of home of which Dr. Zeller was so fond, is a far more expensive system to maintain than the

Kirkbride model, in which all of the inmates are housed in one large building. The state cut funding to the hospital by increments, effectively a "death by a thousand cuts" for the asylum. The number of nurses dwindled, from two thousand to fifteen hundred, down to four hundred. Four hundred attendants to care for four thousand patients. The unparalleled nursing school in the Bowen Building had to close. The nurses had their hands full just trying to give their charges the most basic level of care.

With caregivers scrambling to keep up, even as their numbers dwindled, neglect crept in. Patients could no longer be monitored as closely as they had been in the past. Without supervision, patients wandered the halls of the hospital in various stages of undress. Pepper Bauer, a local author, told me that when she attended Limestone High School in the late 1960s, her church choir went caroling one Christmas. One of their stops was the Peoria State Hospital.

"The patients weren't sitting in chairs for the performance. They were just allowed to wander around, and yeah, some of them weren't entirely dressed, you know. I remember that we were in a big room with green walls, with what seemed like one little 40-watt bulb to light it. There was one guy who just stood really close to me, staring at me the whole time I was singing."

In 1989, the Peoria-area reporter Rick Baker posthumously published a book entitled *Mary, Me: In Search of a Lost Lifetime*. It was a scathing indictment of conditions at the Peoria State Hospital at the time of its closing in 1973. The book focused on one inmate, a woman who had been found wandering along a northern Illinois road in the 1930s, suffering from amnesia. She never recovered her memory, or her identity. She died in a nursing home before Baker had even heard her story. But by doing detective work that would make Sherlock Holmes proud, Baker was able to piece together her (probable) history.

Baker's book is fascinating, and notable for the contempt it has for the Peoria State Hospital. Baker admits that the state hospital was one of the most progressive asylums in the world. However, he uses only two sentences to describe the caring legacy of Dr. Zeller. The rest of that entire chapter is devoted to detailing the horrific conditions of life in the asylum, calling it "an overpopulated, understaffed, antiquated murderous pile of infection … a nightmare where people sat with large, open sores, eating their own feces … (it) stood on the hills near the river like some once great mastodon being devoured by parasites". Powerful words, indeed. The book is worth reading for the guilty pleasure of its delicious shock value. But how much of it is true? And how much of it is one man's opinion, skewed by a journalist to make sensational reading?

Another reporter for the *Peoria Journal Star,* Phil Luciano, has casually referred to the hospital as "the hellhole on the hill". Years later, though, he wrote a compassionate, lovely article about Mattie Sutton, who is working tirelessly to restore the cemeteries at the asylum. I tried several times to contact Luciano for this book, but I could not get him to return my phone calls or my emails. I was intensely curious to know what had made him change his mind about the asylum.

Some people still practically turn their head and spit whenever the asylum in Bartonville is mentioned. What is the reason behind this knee-jerk animosity? How did the Peoria State Hospital go from being a model of modern psychiatric treatment, famous worldwide for its revolutionary methods and for the compassionate care shown its patients, to being reviled as "the hellhole on the hill"?

The asylum has been closed for decades. The windows of the Bowen Building are mostly broken out, the roof falling in, the floors dangerously weakened from exposure to years of Illinois weather. Raccoons make their nests in the walls of the Pollak Hospital. The soaring space of the gymnasium now echoes with the twang of country music. The experiences of the patients, for good or ill, are now a part of the past, a lifetime away. The institution of the Peoria State Hospital can no longer defend itself.

So why the continued revulsion? I think it's just a sane person's terror of imagining finding himself in a place like that unnecessarily. We hear stories today about the asylums of the past, when people were admitted for epilepsy or alcoholism, for medical reasons that had nothing to do with mental illness. We hear about inmates being committed for trivial things like heat stroke or masturbation or menopause, things that seem like part of everyday life to us now. These certainly don't seem like reasons to lock someone away.

The insane asylum has historically been a place of fear, pain and abuse. Want to make a horror novel twice as horrible? Set it in an asylum. The backstory of one of the scariest monsters in movie history, Freddie Krueger, includes his origin as the product of gang rape in the dark, dingy hallways of a mental hospital. Every horror movie aficionado knows instinctively, if a story takes place in an asylum, nothing good's going to come of it. There will be no redemption, no happy ending. There will be blood, and filth, and pain, and tears. Horror novels are the same way. Setting a novel in an asylum is a surefire recipe for desperate fear.

Even real life reflects this. In the bibliography of this book, there are several resources that describe the pain and horror of life behind the bars of the asylum. The horror continues today, with accounts like Susanna Kaysen's *Girl, Interrupted.* The stigma of the asylum, and the fear of being committed, of being locked up, of having one's freedom taken away, haunt us to this day.

But the Peoria State Hospital was nothing like that. For most of its existence, it was held up to the rest of the country as a model of what psychiatric treatment *could* be. It was used as an example of what could be achieved with kind words, gentle treatment, the total absence of restraints, healthy food, wholesome entertainment, and productive work. I spoke with several people whose relatives spent time as patients at the Peoria State Hospital. Their stories are included in the next chapter. I found it interesting that out of all the people I talked to, only one mentioned that conditions at the asylum were anything less than pleasant. (The one exception was Pepper's story about performing with her church choir for the patients.) I don't know if they were recalling only good memories about their relatives, or if time had softened the edges of their recollections. It's true that the people I spoke with were simply weekend visitors to the hospital, not patients. They were mostly quite young, children taken to visit "Uncle Jeffery" on a Sunday afternoon. But children are perceptive. Not a single one of the people who shared their memories with me told of horrible conditions at the asylum.

As for myself, the more I learn about conditions at other hospitals, the more I am filled with an intense gratitude that the Peoria State Hospital was nothing like that. Accounts of life at other institutions tell of cold showers, where the water was poured on the patient from a height of eighteen feet. Photographs taken at the Peoria State Hospital show patients standing for their therapeutic shower under a shower head placed at a perfectly normal height. At other asylums, patients were forced into cage-like boxes, trapped in straightjackets, and locked away from the world behind iron bars. At Peoria State Hospital, Rhoda Derry, who had spent most of the previous forty-three years locked in a box bed, was allowed to stretch her pale, spindly limbs in a real bed with clean sheets. Straightjackets and manacles were banned. Their only use was as museum exhibits, something for the staff at the hospital to point to and say, "Never again. Not here."

Other accounts tell of patients at asylums being force-fed, of having a wedge shoved into their mouths to facilitate medicine dosing, breaking teeth in the process, of the patients in the geriatric ward getting one meal a day, consisting of a thin, colorless broth. At Peoria State Hospital, patients were never restrained. They were fed wholesome food, supplied by the asylum's three farms. Personal accounts of life at other institutions describe the mind-numbing monotony of sitting in a chair staring dully out a window, of not being allowed to do anything that would provide mental or physical stimulation. The days and weeks at Peoria State Hospital were filled with activities. For years, the patients made the clothes that were worn by all the inmates. They were pants and shirts or dresses, too, not the shapeless pajamas we picture when we think of mental patients. The patients attended dances and movies every week. They tended the gardens that produced the food they ate. They raised the chickens and the pigs that provided the eggs and bacon for their breakfasts. They cared for the animals in the zoo – whose fenced-in yard was created from the grates that had formerly barred the windows of the asylum – and trained a tame black bear to take baths in a pool on command. The *patients* did this. These activities were part of their daily life.

At other asylums, patients weren't permitted to have sharp objects, even sewing needles. Dressmaking was out of the question: in addition to being messy, with fabric and patterns spread out all over a room, it also involved the use of scissors. Putting needles and scissors into the hands of insane women? Unthinkable!

One of Dr. Zeller's favorite photographs shows a group of several men, epileptics, standing around a pool table. One of the men is lining up a shot with his cue. It's a perfectly ordinary scene – until you start to think about what it would feel like to be beaten with a pool cue. Or to have a billiard ball slammed into the bridge of your nose. Epileptics who were committed to state hospitals were considered to be potentially, explosively violent. For Dr. Zeller to encourage these men to enjoy a quiet game of pool was revolutionary. This photograph became one of Dr. Zeller's favorite examples of the effectiveness of his treatment.

That treatment, for the most part, was simple kindness.

Dr. George Zeller had every right to be proud of that photograph. It represented the vindication of his beliefs, that the mentally ill were still human beings, exactly like those who cared for them. One of Dr. Zeller's first acts as superintendent of the asylum was to get the name changed, from the Illinois Asylum for the Incurable Insane to Peoria State Hospital. The original name offended him. His attitude towards mental health was this: "Don't tell my patients they can't be cured. I'm here to do just that."

The Peoria State Hospital was the only asylum to send social workers to the homes of the patients, to see if it was the situation in the household that was making the patient crazy. The Peoria State Hospital had the highest rate of reintegration into society, due largely to this practice of follow-up home visits.

The asylum served not only the insane of the state of Illinois, but also the ill and needy of the surrounding communities. The Leviton and Talcott Hospitals, and later, the Pollak Hospital, opened their doors to any member of the community that needed care, no matter their ability to pay. The Leviton and the Talcott provided medical tests and surgeries, while the Pollak served as a tuberculosis ward.

Dr. Zeller himself was a military man to his employees, but a father figure to his patients. Dr. Zeller refused to hire what he called "bug housers", any attendant who had previously worked in an asylum before coming to the hilltop. If he found that a bug houser had slipped past the application process, he would fire that staff member immediately and without cause. But Dr. Zeller also lobbied the state senate for an eight-hour workday. He realized that working more than eight hours at a stretch was harmful to his staff's mental health.

There is a wonderful photograph of Dr. Zeller in the asylum archives. It shows Dr. Zeller, his bearing military-stiff, standing with several attendants in a field. It is only with a second look that you can see the two hundred patients sitting quietly behind Dr. Zeller, partially hidden in the tall grass in the field. When Dr. Zeller went for a walk, the patients went with him. He just had that sort of charisma. In the early days, before the gymnasium was built, before the bars on the windows were turned into paddocks for deer, before the dances and films and visits from the circus, the only activity available to the patients was a stroll outdoors – or rather, a hike. The reasoning behind this was simple: a tired patient was a quiet patient.

The Peoria State Hospital was inspected every three months by a group from the village of Bartonville and the state of Illinois. Dr. Zeller welcomed these visits, as they gave him and his staff the chance to show the good they were doing. Dr. Zeller also encouraged the press to visit the asylum as often as they liked, in search of stories. He believed in complete transparency.

The staff of doctors, nurses, and attendants at the Peoria State Hospital had every right to be proud of the institution where they worked. It was *not* a place of terror and despair. It was a place of caring. It was a place of healing those who could be healed. And for those who were beyond healing, those who would never rejoin society, it was a place of refuge. At the asylum, minds too badly damaged ever to become functional were met with kindness. The tuberculosis patients were cared for with compassion until they died. And the mentally ill were allowed to mingle with others who were like them. Fractured spirits met kindred spirits, and found comfort.

# LIFE AT THE PEORIA STATE HOSPITAL

*"Our biggest fear is that Doc Zeller may make being insane a pleasure." – an Illinois senator, quoted in a newspaper article about the Peoria State Hospital*

Imagine, just for a moment, that you are insane.

Maybe you're depressed. Maybe things just haven't gone your way for a very long time. Maybe your life just seems kind of ... bleak.

Maybe you can't seem to make it through the day without a glass of wine, or two, or five. Or maybe you need something a little harder to keep the shakes at bay. Maybe you're epileptic, just waiting for the next lightning strike to hit your brain.

Or maybe, things are worse than that. Maybe there are so many voices in your head, you're no longer sure which voice is your own. Maybe you can't make your way through the rusty fishhooks and barbed wire in your mind any more. Maybe it hurts so bad to be you that you just can't stand it.

You know you need help, but you've heard such horror stories about almshouses. You don't want to be bound, helpless, in a straitjacket.

You're terrified of ending up shackled to a bed, trapped in a room just as your mind is trapped in the bony prison of your skull.

But there is hope.

There is the Peoria State Hospital.

Life at the Peoria State Hospital was as close to normal as it could possibly be. Patients lived in cottages together, spending most of their time with people who understood them. Epileptics lived with other epileptics, using the buddy system – they were paired off, and each patient kept an eye on his or her partner. If an epileptic patient suffered a seizure, help was as close as their buddy.

Alcoholics were assigned to work with other alcoholics, in the cottages on D Row. This system had another underlying benefit beyond simple camaraderie. Alcoholics who had dried out and were able to function were assigned to care for the new arrivals, the patients who were still suffering in the grip of the terrible shakes and sickness and hallucinations of the DTs. This reminded the more stable patients of where they'd come from – and where they could end up once again if they ever found themselves backsliding into the bottle.

Dr. Zeller was the first to recognize that service veterans who had seen combat sometimes suffered from a tortuous mental illness. We now call that illness "post traumatic stress disorder". Dr. Zeller assigned these veterans to their own cottage, where they could fight their demons in peace. Veterans also had their own burying grounds as a mark of respect for their service.

Dr. Zeller also recognized that some women, after giving birth, suffered from issues ranging from depression to violence against their newborn children. He assigned them to their own cottage as well. In recognizing postpartum depression as a stress disorder, he saved many young women from death sentences. Dr. Zeller found many of these women in prisons, where they'd been locked up for attacking their children or their husbands. The courts found these women "criminally insane", and sentenced many to die for their violent crimes. Dr. Zeller brought them to the Peoria State Hospital. He saved their sanity – and he saved their lives.

Most of the patients on the hilltop weren't violent, though. During the seventy-one years of the asylum's operation, there were only seven murders there. This is a much lower murder rate than most small towns. There were only two violent wards on the hilltop, in C Row; one for men, the other for women. These were the only wards which were regularly locked.

Patients were encouraged to socialize, to the extent that their issues allowed them to do so. Patients took their breakfast and lunch in their cottages, but they all came together for dinner in the Dining Hall.

Shared mealtimes were not the only way that the staff encouraged socialization. The cottages were decorated for every holiday and for every patient's birthday. There were dances every Friday night, and movies every Saturday night. These were held in what is now Stone Country. The attendants took a group of patients to see the Barnum and Bailey Circus one year, in Peoria. The proprietors of the circus were so impressed with the patients' good behavior that the next year, when they came to the area, they set up on the grounds of the asylum for a performance.

There is a fascinating video clip, filmed in the later years of the asylum's operation, that shows inmates playing "donkey baseball". Seriously. The players would hit the ball, then hop on the back of a donkey and try, hilariously, to make it to first base without getting bucked off.

The hilltop was a self-sufficient community. Farms provided the food for both patients and staff, over five hundred acres. (One of the huge gardens, located down the road that now runs past the Alpha Park Library, is now a Peoria Police Benevolent Property, and is used as a recreational area.) Farms and gardens alike were tended by patients. The staff felt that caring for chickens and other small animals gave the patients a sense of responsibility. Each cottage was assigned a chicken pen, and this practice turned out to be especially therapeutic for violent patients. Dr. Zeller wrote in his memoirs about a particular patient who suffered from paranoid dementia, who was completely cured and allowed to go home. Before she left the asylum, she spoke with Dr. Zeller, who asked what had brought her mind back to reason. The woman said it was the chirp of the chicks, which were outside when a storm blew into the area. She hurried to catch the chicks and bring them to safe shelter, and that's when it occurred to her that they were tiny, helpless creatures who needed her protection. "This woman, who smashed furniture and tore clothes became a ministering angel to a brood of helpless chicks," Dr. Zeller marveled.

The patients also made their own clothes; pants, dresses, underwear, everything except shoes. When the clothes wore out, patients tore the rags into strips and wove them into carpets. (Locally grown food, self-sufficiency, recycling – sounds pretty modern, right? Yeah. This was in 1908.)

The patients were also allowed visitors. A bus ran up the hill six times a day, bringing visitors to see their loved ones. A lot of the people I spoke with about the asylum told of visiting relatives. One woman told me about going to visit her Uncle Bill in the "bughouse". She was three or four years old at the time, but her memories of the visits are vivid.

"Uncle Bill was a radar tech in the Navy. After he was released from the asylum, he actually went back and worked at a military base. When one of his children was born, my little cousin, it was Bill who suffered from postpartum depression, not his wife. It was his sixth kid, and it just got to be a little much for him. He jumped into the baby's playpen and spilled red ink all over my cousin's diapers.

"This worried my grandfather, so he committed Uncle Bill. His own father committed him. I guess he did some other violent things too.

"Uncle Bill worked in the kitchen at the asylum. I remember going to visit him on Sundays, and he would take us back into the kitchen to show us where he worked. There was this big, tall green curtain. He would take hold of the edge of the curtain, and draw it aside with a grand flourish. There behind the curtain was the egg room. I always thought it was funny – here Uncle Bill was such a violent guy, and what do they put him in charge of? The eggs."

Elizabeth Bigger shared a story that her father, a plasterer, had told her. He had served his apprenticeship at the asylum. One summer, his job was to fill holes in the bathroom walls. One woman, he said, would follow behind him as he worked, scraping the fresh plaster out with her fingers. He just shrugged and called it "job security".

A gentleman I met in Glasford told me that he'd played in a softball league in the 1950s. The teams were required to play one game a season at the asylum.

"We didn't play the inmates, of course – they were the spectators. The game didn't count for anything in the league scores; we just played for fun. And boy, it was fun. You never knew what was going to happen in those games. One of the inmates might suddenly decide to ride a bike right through the infield while we were playing. Or someone might come out and run around the bases, just because. And all the other inmates watching, they'd just clap and applaud and have a grand old time. It was tons of fun."

Not all of the stories that tell of life in the asylum are so rosy, though. A woman I spoke with, who worked as a student nurse there, was told, "Keep the patients in front of you". The young nurse was in one of the wards when a disturbed patient popped out from behind a pillar and shrieked "You did it!" The patient put her hands in the middle of the nurse's back, shoved, and pushed her down a flight of stairs.

"I never touched another stair," the woman told me. She was saved from injury, though, by another nurse. "She was a bigger girl, and I landed on top of her. She broke my fall."

The same woman told me about caring for another patient. This sweet old lady would sit and knit with her. The young nurse wondered, how could this lady's family commit her to such a place? When she managed to find the patient's history, she learned that this sweet old lady chased her granddaughter around the dining room table with a butcher knife.

Some patients were committed for very good reasons. But everyone who lived at the asylum was treated with dignity and kindness. This is what we need to remember as we explore the darkened hallways and hidden corners of the Peoria State Hospital.

# RUMORS AND TRUTHS

"You know if you go out to the old mental hospital in Bartonville, and your car has any kind of mechanical issues at all, when you go to leave, your car won't start."

"I heard there are bums living in the tunnels under the buildings. A couple of them died down there in the 1980s, and their ghosts still haunt the tunnels."

"Yeah, those tunnels, they were built by the patients. If any of the patients died while they were working, they just walled them up, right there where they fell. Just like the Great Wall of China, man. If you go down in the tunnels, you can see boots sticking out of the walls where the dead patients are buried."

"There are these caves underneath the hospitals, right? And old Dr. Zeller would keep patients down there to box with. All these rich people from Bartonville and Peoria used to come to watch Dr. Zeller beat the crap out of the asylum patients."

"There's a Hanging Tree in the woods next to the Bowen, right there across the street. A bunch of those crazies hung themselves, and you can still see bodies hanging in the trees."

"My friend's cousin went down in the gully down by one of the cemeteries. There are these weird drawings on the rocks. See, they kept the patients chained down in the ravine, and they drew pictures on the rocks 'cause they were crazy. Some of the pictures are of aliens, too. Swear to God. Gotta be, 'cause they've got big heads and skinny little arms."

Within months of the hospital's closing, curiosity seekers moved in on the place. They broke into the locked buildings in search of souvenirs. There was quite a lot to find. When the Peoria State Hospital closed in 1973, the state basically locked the doors and walked away. Everything was simply left behind, exactly as it was when the last nurse closed the doors behind her, went home, and kicked off her crepe-soled shoes. People found beds, plates, clothes, wheelchairs, desks, gurneys, all kinds of *things* just left where people had last laid them down.

They also found ghosts.

As early as the mid-1970s, people knew there was something just a little off about the place, some air of haunted desolation beyond its history as an asylum. The stigma of the asylum was strong, no doubt about that. Parents would threaten unruly children – "Knock off that noise, or I'll pack you up and ship you off to Bartonville!" Family members that had been committed were spoken of in hushed voices, as though they had contracted some terrible disease. "Uncle Bill's in *the asylum*," people would whisper, in the same low voice they'd have used to say "It's *cancer*."

But the abandoned mental institution held a quiet air of spooky menace beyond its sad state of disuse and disrepair. Shortly after the hospital closed, in the mid-1970s, a few of the cottages were reopened and rented out for craft shows and flea markets. It was quality stuff, too. One woman bought a leather purse at one of these shows for her daughter, who still uses it. She's tickled at the thought that her granddaughter will get it someday.

Some people didn't have such a good time at these weekend jumble sales, though. Dawn Tudor went to an art sale in one of the cottages. She was new to Illinois, and knew absolutely nothing about the history of the building. She had heard there was to be an art and antique sale to benefit some charity or other, and she came to Bartonville to check it out. She walked into one of the cottages, and was drawn to a teddy bear that sat in a chair halfway down the hall.

She took ten steps down the hallway, and then had to turn around and leave.

"Bad vibes," was her only explanation. "I just didn't feel it was a safe environment. I just decided I was leaving, and I was not going back in."

She never did go back to buy the teddy bear she'd wanted so much.

Those cottages were the first buildings to come down when the demolition of the hospital began. The city of Bartonville tried for years to sell them. But the dormitories were too small for any sort of industrial use, and no one wanted to live in the cottages because of the lingering stigma of the asylum. So the buildings were simply knocked over – the entire structure pushed with bulldozers into the hole that had been the basement.

One of these cottages does survive. There was a special cottage, one of the smaller ones, set aside for patients who were also veterans. (The veterans had their own burying ground as well, the GAR cemetery located in Cemetery 1.) Luckily, the building was spared from the wrecking ball. It's now a dentist's office. The current owners do not like to be associated with the asylum, and they do not welcome the curious.

Many of the rumors swirl around the tunnel system, mostly because tunnels are such dark, spooky places to begin with. I was talking with a ghost hunter at Bartonville, and we happened to be standing next to a wooden walkway. The ghost hunter said, "Wanna see something cool?" Then he reached down and heaved up a section of the walkway. Rusty metal steps, hidden by a deep drift of dry leaves, led down into the blackness. I fumbled my keychain flashlight out of my pocket, but the tiny light did nothing to push back that oppressive dark.

"The first time I opened this," he said, "I was hit with this wave of sadness. All the spirits down there bumrushed me. Every hair on my arms was sticking straight up."

These dark tunnels are rumored to hold their secrets. People were moved from building to building using the tunnels, like herding sheep underground. Homeless bums died down there in the blackness. There was one tunnel leading from the asylum down to the Illinois River, and the nurses took uncooperative patients down to the river and drowned them.

None of these tales are true, of course. The reality is much more prosaic. No one was allowed to go down into the tunnels except for workers doing maintenance. The hilltop had its own powerhouse, its own water treatment plant, all the basics needed to supply a small town. The tunnels formed a maintenance system for all the underground utilities.

But what kind of storytellers would we be if we only told the truth?

The National Guard unit in Bartonville used to use the tunnels for their exercises. A friend of mine told me that he knew a guy in the Guard that was terrified of the dark. His buddies knew about this, and they'd prank the guy unmercifully. They'd wait until the whole group was in the middle of the tunnel system, then everyone would turn out their flashlights and stomp on the floor, making the noise of their combat boots sound fainter and fainter, as if the group was running away and leaving this poor schmuck behind in the dark. (His own flashlight had been sabotaged – outfitted with dead batteries, courtesy of his buddies.) This poor guy would get so freaked out that he'd run – usually smack into the tunnel wall. He cold-cocked himself a couple of times. They managed to "get" this guy three times in about five minutes – he kept on falling for the same gag.

(To be honest, the guy kind of deserved it. Ed Hanley, who knew this poor schmuck, told me that this dude had been telling everyone stories about the scary homeless people living in the tunnels. Well, it was getting irritating, the way the guy kept going on and on. So Ed and his friend Dean decided to teach this guy a lesson. Ed and Dean snuck into the morgue. There were four body drawers in the wall, and a heap of castoff clothes moldering in the corner. Ed ran a length of wire through the clothes, wiring them together, and stuffed the whole thing into one of the drawers. Then he and Dean got the whole group together. All the guys were in on the gag, except the victim. The group herded this guy into the morgue and stood there, unobtrusively blocking the door. Ed asked, "What's the matter – you scared? Here," and opened one of the non-rigged drawers, showing it to be empty. The chances were now one in three that the next drawer opened would be the one with the manky clothes in it. The guy, baited by the group, yanked open the rigged drawer, and the bundle of stinky clothes leapt onto his face. The guy clawed the moldy fabric off of his face, wheeled around, and practically climbed over the wall of bodies in his hurry to get out of the morgue.)

It is sadly true that a patient from the cottage that housed the depression cases wandered away from his cottage and hanged himself in the woods. Over the next few months, two more depressed patients followed his example. But these were copycat suicides. The hangings were a tragedy, but they were an isolated occurrence. There was no "Hanging Tree" in the woods near the Bowen.

The cemeteries are another rich mine of rumors. If it rains real hard, there are washouts at the edges of the cemeteries next to the ravines, and bodies wash out of their graves into the ravines. You can still find bones down in the ravines, it's true. There's also a "dirty babies" area where stillbirths, miscarriages, and abortions were buried. It's not registered as a cemetery, but there are documents saying that the city has to parcel that area off, and they have to mow that area at the same time they mow the cemeteries. And speaking of abortions, the doctors at the asylum used to perform abortions down in the ravines, and they buried the babies down there too. You can't have crazy women having babies.

All of this, of course, is complete nonsense. There have been washouts at the edge of the cemetery next to the ravine that wanders through the bluff top. But even with a heavy downpour, the worst erosion that could possibly happen would be that the top few inches of topsoil would be washed away. Hardly a threat to a body buried six feet deep. Besides, these patients were fed three meals a day of healthy food, most of it raised in the gardens and on the farms right there on the hospital grounds. When they died, they were buried in simple pine boxes, with no embalming. The pine box would rot, forming a pocket of acidic soil around the decomposing body. In the rich, dark soil of this part of Illinois, it only takes eight to twelve years to reduce a body to teeth and bone chips. The last burial on the hilltop took place right at the time the asylum closed, in 1973. That was four decades ago. Any bodies buried in the cemeteries have long ago returned to the earth. You can find bones in the ravines, but they're much more likely to belong to a deer than to a human being. The leg bones or ribs of a deer can look alarmingly human. Bored gravediggers on their breaks are responsible for the pecked stone art found on the boulders at the top of the ravine.

As for the rumors of abortions being performed in the ravines – well, there are some people in this world that have very vivid imaginations.

Babies were welcomed at the Peoria State Hospital. Dr. Zeller firmly believed that a child should be allowed to stay with its mother. Even the criminally insane women who were temporarily housed in the Bowen Building were allowed to keep their children with them until the child turned four years old.

The "dirty babies area" is actually a slag pit left over from the days when Bartonville was home to a village of coal miners. The corrugated, bumpy soil is simply where the waste from the mines was dumped. The reason the city mows the area is because there's an old pump house there. The pathway to the pump house needs to be kept maintained. The rumors of a "hidden" cemetery may also refer to a graveyard that served the coal miners' settlement.

There are so many rumors that swirl around the old asylum, like dust kicked up during an Illinois windstorm in the spring. The rumors can fly thick and fast, obscuring the truth about life at the asylum. But if we wait for the dust to settle, we can begin to see the facts more clearly.

And the facts, at the Peoria State Hospital, are often just as fascinating as the rumors.

# PEOPLE OF THE PEORIA STATE HOSPITAL

*"It was awful but it was real. I saw it. One hundred nurses and 300 spectators saw it."*

*Dr. George Zeller, writing of Old Book's funeral*

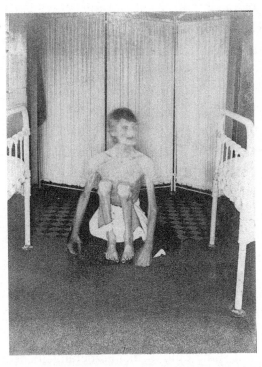

*Rhoda Derry*

She looks inhuman, like a withered gargoyle crouched on the floor, or a pale, living mummy, skinny beyond any human comprehension but alive, impossibly alive. The primitive camera of the early twentieth century has captured her just as she turns, so her face is a smudgy blur. But the hollow eyes still haunt us from a distance of over a century. (Photograph courtesy of Richard Weiss.)

The story of Rhoda Derry is one of the great tragedies and one of the great triumphs of Dr. Zeller's career. Rhoda was born in 1840 in Adams County, Illinois, the daughter of a prosperous farmer. She grew up privileged, and was strikingly beautiful, so they say. While still in her teens, she was courted by the son of a family that lived on a nearby farm. The young man's mother, though, was adamantly opposed to the match. She came to see Rhoda and threatened to curse her if Rhoda didn't break off the engagement at once.

We have no way of knowing, a century and a half later, how far the relationship had gone by then. All we know is that Rhoda and her young beau were engaged. Rhoda had found someone she loved so much that when he asked her to marry him, she said yes. Had it gone any farther than that? Had they even kissed? We don't know.

But the young man's mother threatened to curse Rhoda if she didn't release the man from their engagement. Did Rhoda refuse? Was there a screaming match between Rhoda and her almost-future-mother in law? Did she knuckle under instead, silently seething with resentment? Again, we'll never know.

The power of suggestion, though, is a strange and insidious thing. Shortly after the young man's mother made the threat, Rhoda started showing signs of a woman possessed. She came home one day, jumped up on the bed, and started spinning around on her head, saying that "Old Scratch" was after her. This psychotic break marked the beginning of Rhoda's sharp decline. Her relatives cared for her as long as they could. Eventually, though, they committed her to the Adams County almshouse when she was in her early thirties.

Rhoda was a difficult patient. She would shove food into her mouth at mealtimes, not bothering with the niceties of a fork or spoon. While in the grip of her madness, she clawed her own eyes out. She also knocked out all of her teeth. Was it some kind of mental derangement that caused this destructive behavior? Was it heartbreak over her lost love, a life of happiness and contentment forcibly taken from her? Was her mind reacting to the threat of black magic with a very real self-destruction? Once again, we will never know the secrets that were locked away in Rhoda's tortured soul. The hellish part of it is that her almost-mother-in-law actually came to visit her during this time. The woman tried to apologize to Rhoda, to tell her that there had been no curse, no witchcraft used against her. But Rhoda's mind was too far gone to be retrieved.

Rhoda spent forty-three years at the Adams County almshouse. For much of that time, she was locked in a box bed, a cramped cradle in which she huddled, trying to escape the demons of her own mind. At first, Rhoda was confined to a Utica crib, a coffin-sized cage, lined with straw. Mice made their nests in the straw, and ran over her, their tiny clawed feet tickling as they scurried. The crib had a metal pan underneath it to catch waste, that could be pulled out and emptied when needed ... exactly like a rabbit cage. When her manic phase eventually calmed, she was moved to the box bed. Eventually, the muscles in her arms and legs atrophied, leaving her permanently curled in a fetal position. She was cared for by other feeble-minded patients. On the rare occasions when she was taken out of the bed, she could no longer stand upright. She crabbed along the floor, using her clenched fists to inch her wasted body forward.

In 1904, Dr. Zeller visited the Adams County almshouse in search of hopeless cases. There, he found Rhoda Derry. He made arrangements to have her transferred to the Peoria State Hospital.

Rhoda arrived at the asylum in the fall of 1904, at the end of a very long day. There had been a washout, so the train coming from Quincy, Illinois, was delayed for several hours. The train finally arrived at one o'clock in the morning. Patients arriving at the train station would be met at the station near the river by hospital attendants. Then they would be escorted up the long staircase that led up the hillside to the bluff top. The staircase is still there today, although its metal handrail is missing in places, and its concrete steps are crumbling badly.

The hospital attendants met the late train, and the new patients stumbled off, yawning and rubbing their eyes. Two attendants grabbed what they assumed was a wicker basket of clothes, and started up the staircase. They got quite the shock – as did everyone else – when the clothes in the basket moved and parted, and Rhoda sat up and began to jabber toothlessly.

(Rhoda, incidentally, was not the only mentally ill patient ever to be carried around in a basket. It was common practice in the almshouses of the day to confine patients in wicker baskets, as well as in box beds and Utica cribs. This is where the phrase "basket case" originated.)

That night, Rhoda slept in a real bed, with clean white sheets, for the first time in forty-three years. The nurses devoted themselves to her care. From the moment she arrived until her death two years later, Rhoda had nurses attending her constantly. She still snatched food that was offered to her and crammed it into her mouth, but she was no longer confined to bed. She was allowed to make her way around a room, crabbing along on the knuckles of her clenched fists, dragging her withered legs behind her. She had a fondness for chewing tobacco, and would pull on people's pants legs to beg for some chaw.

The nurses who cared for her doted on her, treating her "like a daughter", according to Dr. Zeller's memoirs. They would wheel her around outside, letting her experience the hilltop as best she could. After being locked in a box bed for forty-three years, Rhoda felt the sun on her face, and breathed the fresh air of the outdoors. She smelled the flowers in the gardens, and the scent of freshly cut grass. She heard music when the nurses took her to the dance hall. Maybe she swayed her wasted body to the beat, and clapped her withered hands as she grinned in toothless delight. She could no longer see, but she could still hear, and touch, and smell. The nurses made sure she experienced her new home at the Peoria State Hospital to the best of her abilities.

Dr. Zeller never let Rhoda become an object of idle curiosity, even though the circumstances of her arrival in a clothes basket were sensational. Visitors to the Peoria State Hospital were shocked at her condition, of course, and with good reason. But Dr. Zeller insisted that the attendants at the almshouse, who had kept Rhoda confined to the box bed, had really been caring for her the best way they knew how. No one ever blamed her former attendants for her condition, but everyone agreed that the Peoria State Hospital was a world away from the squalor she had endured for over forty years.

And Rhoda apparently recognized Dr. Zeller, and adored him for his kindness. When he entered the room, she knew it, and would smile with excitement. She seemed to be genuinely happy to have him visit her. Did she recognize his voice? The smell of cologne? Who knows? But she knew he was her savior.

Rhoda died in 1906. She is buried in Cemetery 1, the resting place of those whose families could afford a better burial than a narrow pauper's grave. At the end, her family still cared enough about her to give her a decent burial. Rhoda's grave is front and center in the graveyard, only three rows back from the edge of the cemetery nearest the road. Rhoda's stone is still there, although it is not the original. The original was stolen many years ago. A cemetery commission put up a newer stone to mark Rhoda's grave in 1983. Now the grave is marked with an ancient-looking chunk of stone, plus a newer stone, gleaming white with a black metal plaque. A small rock marker, like the kind sold in garden shops to mark the grave of a beloved pet, stands guard as well. The phrase on the smaller marker reads: "Until we meet again, find peace in heaven's hands". A white porcelain cherub blows a kiss to passersby. The plaque dedicated to Rhoda by the cemetery commission reads:

*217*

*Rhoda Derry*

*1840-1906*

*They built this place of asylum so that no*

*other human would suffer as you.*

*You taught us to love and feel*

*compassion towards the less fortunate.*

*May you find peace and warmth in God's arms.*

Rhoda's wasted body was gone, but her spirit survived. For years after her death, nurses reported seeing Rhoda's hunched form sitting on the porch of the cottage where she had spent her last years.

Rhoda's ghost is still around today. She can be felt pretty much anywhere. Rhoda loved the hilltop. Perhaps that's why her spirit manifests in many different places at the asylum. Sharon Wood was standing with a group of ghost hunters near Rhoda's grave one crisp fall night. Sharon felt her necklace lift and stand straight out from her neck, as if someone was picking it up to examine it. She tugged it back down. Rhoda's curiosity wasn't satisfied, though. Sharon's necklace lifted away from her neck twice more as she stood there.

Other people have experienced Rhoda's presence. She likes to tug on people's pants legs to get their attention from where she's sitting hunched on the floor. And sometimes, the strong odor of chewing tobacco will fill the air, as Rhoda begs for a twist of her beloved chaw.

*Old Book*

Early on, a patient was brought to the Peoria State Hospital because he'd had a nervous breakdown at work. He was mute, unable to tell the intake nurses his name. The only thing anyone knew about this fellow was that he had worked in a book bindery in Peoria. His name, therefore, was entered into the ledger as A. Bookbinder (or Manual Bookbinder). He became known familiarly as "Old Book".

Bookbinder was encouraged, as were all the inmates, to find useful work to do at the asylum to keep his mind and body occupied. It became Book's chore to dig graves for the patients who died, and to care for the cemeteries on the hilltop. Book also attended each funeral that took place on the grounds. (The film about Old Book that was produced by Reality's End Films fancifully has Rhoda's funeral as the first one Book attended. The timing is right, but we have no way of knowing that Book actually dug Rhoda's grave, or attended her funeral.)

At the first funeral he attended, Book was standing next to the grave, and his shoulders began to hitch. Tears leaked from his eyes and tracked silently down his cheeks. A sob escaped him, and he walked over to the large tree that stood in the middle of the cemetery. He leaned against the trunk of the tree and wailed, crying as if his heart was breaking. When the short service was over, he collected himself and came back to fill in the grave. Old Book did this at every funeral he attended as gravedigger.

In 1910, Old Book himself passed away. He may have died of tuberculosis. (The Reality's End production also describes Book as having a red handkerchief. Patients suffering with TB were often given a red handkerchief, to hide the fact that they were, at the end, coughing up blood. While there is a record in the asylum's account books that Bookbinder did purchase two handkerchiefs, there is no mention of the color.) Bookbinder did die at the height of one of the pellagra outbreaks at the asylum, so that may have been the cause of his death.

All of the patients on the hilltop were respected as individuals, and Old Book was quite the character. So his funeral was well attended. The mourners sang a hymn – perhaps there were a few tears for Book, knowing that he would never again lean against the trunk of the Graveyard Elm and weep for those who had passed on. Then the pallbearers, four large men, each grabbed the ends of the ropes that supported the coffin, preparing to lower it into the ground.

The men heaved – and the coffin bounced up under their effort as if it was empty! The crowd gasped, and everyone took a step back in confusion. Suddenly everyone heard an agonized wailing coming from the Graveyard Elm. The phantom of Old Book stood there, leaning against the tree, crying and sobbing just as he had for so many others.

Some spectators ran from the scene. Some slumped to the ground when their knees buckled and they tried to take in the sight of the weeping spirit. Dr. Zeller marched over to the coffin and ordered it to be opened. The pallbearers pried open the coffin and lifted the lid – and in that instant the wailing stopped. Old Book lay there in his coffin, sleeping peacefully – and unquestionably dead.

Dr. Zeller wrote about this frightening incident in his memoirs. He wrote: "It was awful but it was real. I saw it. One hundred nurses and three hundred spectators saw it."

The story doesn't end there. A few years later, the Graveyard Elm began to die. Dr. Zeller feared that branches from the dying tree would fall and injure someone, or damage the headstones underneath it. So he sent a work crew out to chop it down. As the first stroke of the ax fell, though, the tree trunk seemed to shudder, and a wailing came from the tree. The voice sounded remarkably like Old Book. The workmen threw their axes down and refused to continue.

Dr. Zeller then sent out a crew of firemen to do a controlled burn to take out the tree. The firemen came out to the cemetery and piled kindling all around the base of the tree. As soon as they lit it, the crying rose again from the tree's trunk, and the face of Old Book seemed to swirl in the smoke. The firemen put out the burn and gave up.

The Graveyard Elm eventually died on its own, and fell. The tree's massive trunk was pushed into the ravine that rings the cemetery, and eventually rotted away. The trees that dot the cemetery today are descendants of the Graveyard Elm. They were mere saplings at the time Old Book shed his final tear. Now they stand tall and proud, keeping watch over Old Book and the rest of the sleepers in Cemetery 2 at the Peoria State Hospital.

A cemetery commission was formed in 1983 for the preservation of the burying grounds of the asylum. Their main task was to pull headstones out of the ravines where they'd been dropped by vandals, and to find the proper marker for graves that lacked their stones. The commission also provided modern markers for Rhoda Derry and for Bookbinder. Bookbinder's marker reads:

*713*

*Manual Bookbinder*

*AKA A. Bookbinder*

*1878-1910*

*In each death he found great sorrow.*

*He wept at each passing tears for*

*the unloved and forgotten.*

*Now, "OLD BOOK" we weep for you.*

*"When the moon is full and the sky is clear, you're gonna see shadows." – Brian Fengel, Bartonville chief of police*

In the years since the Peoria State Hospital closed, the remaining buildings – particularly the Bowen Building – have become a magnet for curiosity seekers. With everything just left in place, the asylum was downright irresistible. People broke into the buildings in the dead of night and explored to their curiosity's content.

Unfortunately, not all of the adventurers were respectful of the property which now belonged to the village of Bartonville. The homeless broke in seeking shelter from the weather. Teenagers smuggled in sixpacks. Vandals graffitied the walls, scrawling obscenities in dripping spray paint. The place was already getting a reputation as a haunted hotspot, so the graffiti included arcane symbols, inverted pentagrams, and other references to the Dark Side.

The Bartonville police force soon had their hands full patrolling the asylum grounds. Tales of adventure and exploration always came tempered with the warning: watch out for cops.

Brian Fengel became chief of police of the Bartonville force in 1998. I spoke with him to get his take on the haunted attraction on his beat.

"When the moon is full and the sky is clear, you're gonna see shadows," Fengel said. He's been in those buildings at all hours of the day and night.

"If you're in a building at three in the morning, and it's all dark and quiet, are you going to hear noises? Of course you are. But whether or not those noises are ghosts ..." His voice trailed off, and I could hear the hardnosed, no-nonsense police officer in his tone. He didn't want to disappoint the lady author. But at the same time, he's the chief of police. He's not going to want to say he saw something when he's not sure of what he saw.

Rhonda Wolfe is the mayor of Bartonville. Her foremost concerns are the health of her constituents and the fiscal well-being of the town she loves.

"They want to turn that building into a haunted house." There was a thin, bitter twist of disbelief in her voice as she spoke about the Bowen. "That's not why I wanted to abate the building."

Wolfe is completely, one hundred percent behind the idea of getting the Bowen Building abated. It's for health reasons, she explained. The windows are broken out, exposing the rot inside to the elements. The asbestos will need to be dealt with anyway. The TIF funds for the abatement are available now; they need to be used by 2016 or they'll run out.

But she doesn't want to save the Bowen to see it turned into a haunted attraction. She'd rather have it home to a legitimate business, one that has not a whiff of the supernatural about it. The Bowen is a beautiful building, she said, especially if you go up to the top floor. The views of the Illinois River really are spectacular.

"As far as the 'hauntedness' of it, that's everyone else's opinion," she said. "You're talking to the wrong person... I don't know." Even as she made this flat declaration, though, there was something in her tone, an undercurrent of things left unsaid. I waited patiently.

Wolfe sighed, and even over the phone I could hear a slurry of impatience and bewilderment coating her words. "I'm friends with Gary Lisman, and I went up to the Bowen with him once. It was a chilly day, in the forties, and Gary asked, 'Do you want to come inside?' It turned out to be about ten degrees colder inside the building than it was outside. I had to put my gloves on.

"I wear transition glasses – I can't see without them – but when we went inside the building, the lenses never transitioned back to clear. I couldn't even go up the stairs because my glasses were so dark. They never did get clear, the whole time we were inside."

There are many, many people who love the Peoria State Hospital with a passion. These people volunteer countless hours to keeping up the grounds, helping to run events at the remaining historical buildings, and making themselves available to the curious public. Volunteers help organize ghost investigations, run websites, and answer questions from reporters, writers, television show hosts, and people who are just plain curious about the history and the hauntings at the asylum.

The unofficial historian of the Peoria State Hospital is Chris Morris. She has been fascinated by the asylum since childhood. That obsession has grown into a passion for the asylum and its history.

"I started coming to the hilltop when I was seven years old. My grandfather used to bring me here to visit the cemetery, because a relative of mine is buried here. That was in 1980, and of course the hospital was closed by then.

"My grandfather always told me that this place was a village of 'special people'. Well, I was just a little kid then. I saw the big stone Bowen Building, and I thought he meant it was a town full of giants." Chris chuckled softly at the fanciful ways a child can misinterpret the world. "It was just after the seventies, and people still whispered the name *Bartonville*. There was such a stigma attached to the place.

"Later, I heard stories about the asylum – patients chained to the walls, all that stuff. I knew there had to be more to the place than that. I wanted to know the history, the facts behind the wild stories. The facts don't lie. *History* doesn't lie."

As a teenager, Chris spent countless hours on the hilltop, exploring the tunnels and any building she could get into. She has pored over every photograph ever taken of the grounds, the buildings, the people of the asylum. She has immersed herself in the history – and the hauntings. As a result, she has become a walking, talking encyclopedia of the Peoria State Hospital. She is also one of its staunchest supporters, because she has made it her business to know the truth.

"See this?" she asked. We were sitting in the office at the Pollak Hospital. She held up a manila folder. It was about an inch and a half thick, crammed with newspaper clippings that threatened to spill out from between her fingers. "Here's the good stuff. Here's everything the local papers printed about us, how much food we produced on the hilltop, the movies every Friday night, the dances every Saturday night, the Boy Scout campouts, the time the Barnum and Bailey Circus came and set up on the lawn here."

She put the folder down with a heavy thump on the desk, and picked up a slim sheaf of paper, less than a dozen pages. "And this is the bad stuff." Chris will admit that there were mishaps at the hospital. With the advent of steam heating to heat the therapeutic baths, three patients were accidentally scalded to death. Chris tells the story to visitors calmly. She refuses to sensationalize the tragedies of the asylum's long history. But she is also quick to defend her beloved hilltop.

Chris has immersed herself in the Peoria State Hospital for so long that it seems to have become a part of her. When she speaks, it's hard to realize that she hasn't been here all along, a part of the asylum since its founding.

# GHOST HUNTING

*"When are we going to get started?"* *"Right after the commercial break."*

So why is the hilltop at Bartonville so incredibly haunted? That's a question paranormal investigators have been asking for years. There is a confluence of factors that make this bluff top one of the most haunted places in the United States. It's a perfect storm of paranormal oddities.

Fort Creve Coeur was built in January 1680 by an exploring party of Frenchmen under the leadership of Rene Robert Cavalier, Sieur de la Salle and Henri Tonti. Creve Coeur is north of Bartonville and across the Illinois River. In the records of the fort, one of the officers wrote that the area now known as Bartonville was "the location of an ancient village". It's not clear whether this refers to an actual Native American encampment that was thriving at the time, or to a former village site, or to a burial ground. Research is, unfortunately, inconclusive. Investigators on the hilltop have, however, collected several intriguing EVPs that point to the presence of Native American spirits. The sounds of drumming and chanting have been recorded, as well as fragments of what sounds like speech in a native dialect.

Millions of years before Native Americans made the trek across the Bering Strait, what we know now as the Midwest was covered by an immense shallow inland sea. When the waters receded, they left behind the microscopic shells and skeletons of billions upon billions of tiny marine organisms. This organic detritus formed huge deposits of sedimentary rock. Limestone is created from the deaths of tiny living organisms, whose skeletons form the calcium-rich matrix of the rock.

The world of the paranormal seems to have a particular affinity for this organically created substance. EVPs seem to be especially strong in locations that incorporate a lot of limestone, or in which limestone forms the bedrock under the soil. Light anomalies seem to be more common in these locations too. Limestone may be very good at storing residual psychic energy in ways that we don't fully understand.

If you look at folklore and magickal practices, you find that limestone is believed by many practitioners to be an "energy enhancer". It's often added to spells or rituals to increase the power of the working. Limestone is also used in some kinds of magick to "capture" spirits. Some native traditions also hold that spirits have the ability to "live" in limestone.

The Bowen Building's gorgeous bones are carved from limestone from the oldest quarry of the United States. You can still see the tailings, chips of light-colored stone that line the bottoms of shallow pits scattered around the grounds of the asylum.

When you have water flowing through limestone, whatever vibrations there are seem to be amplified. What runs just a few hundred yards away from the hilltop? The Illinois River, the longest river in the state. Water flows through the ravines after heavy rains as well, and the hilltop is honeycombed with natural springs.

Prehistoric native presence, a matrix of microscopic once-living creatures, the ionization effect of running water – all of these factors contribute to the haunting of the hilltop. But the thing that seals the deal for many researchers is the undeniable presence of the patients.

When the Peoria State Hospital closed its doors in 1973, everything was abandoned, left exactly as it was. Plates were left in cabinets and on tables, waiting for food that would no longer be served. Pianos stood unplayed in the dayrooms of the cottages. Sheets were no longer warmed by bodies at night; pillows no longer bore the imprints of sleeping heads. Clothing, silverware, milk pitchers, books, photographs – everything was just left in place. The people that had once lived in the cottages were gone, either dead or moved to other institutions.

A few curiosity seekers went through looking for souvenirs, but mostly, the cottages were left alone. The taboo of mental illness was too strong of a deterrent. The living wanted nothing to do with these artifacts.

It was up to the dead to reclaim their former lives.

The atmosphere was ripe for spirits to flock to the hilltop. This had been their home for so many years. This was where so many patients found peace and acceptance. It's no wonder that the majority of the spirits people encounter here are the ghosts of patients rather than the ghosts of doctors or nurses. Obviously, there were many more patient deaths here than staff – Dr. Zeller died in his apartment in the Bowen Building in 1938, and Anne Stuart may have died there as well, but those are the only deaths of health care professionals that we can document. Many researchers feel that the spirits are drawn here because the patients felt that the Peoria State Hospital was their home, a place of refuge from the big, confusing world beyond the bluff top. Some of them were of limited intelligence. One of the heartbreaking stories of the asylum's closing tells of a patient who was relocated to another institution in Galesburg, about an hour's drive to the west. The patient escaped and made his way back to Bartonville. A staff member found the patient sitting on the steps of one of the cottages, waiting forlornly to be let back into his old home.

## Equipment and Techniques

Paranormal investigators are, to put it simply, some weird folks. These are the people that hang out in cemeteries in the dead of night, or wander around haunted buildings, with the purpose of tracking ghosts in the most scientific way they can. They try, as much as possible, to focus on quantifiable proof. That being said, there's a bit of the thrill-seeker in every ghost hunter, no matter how much they rely on their instruments. The Peoria State Hospital is such a hotspot of activity that it draws ghost hunting groups from all over the United States, as well as curiosity seekers.

Paranormal researchers and ghost hunters alike use a variety of equipment in their search for evidence of the Other Side. This can be as simple as a flashlight and a small digital voice recorder, as fancy as an infrared camera, or as low-tech as simply paying attention to what's going on around them.

## Cameras

Paranormal investigators have an awfully difficult job. They're trying to capture evidence of the supernatural, something that is by its very nature fluid and nebulous and slippery. They record things they can't hear, and they take pictures of things they can't see.

What investigators do have are theories – ideas, some proven by experience, of how the supernatural world works. One of the fun toys that researchers can play with is an IR (infrared) camera. Investigators know that living people give off a certain amount of thermal energy, heat as a byproduct of our existence in the physical world. They theorize that spirits also give off just a tiny amount of energy – and heat is as good an indicator of that energy as anything else. Heat can be detected in the infrared band. So, if there's a spirit anywhere around, an IR camera might be able to take a picture of it.

There's a neat experiment that high school science teachers like to do. They'll take a volunteer and stand behind her with a colored card, and slowly bring it around her head, asking when the card becomes visible – and then asking when the color of the card can be identified. We can see things in our peripheral vision, but not very clearly, and not in color, which is what the experiment is designed to demonstrate. Since the infrared band is at the lower end of the visual spectrum, this might explain why we catch glimpses of ghosts out of the corners of our eye instead of in a direct line of sight, and why they can appear as gray shadows.

Some amateur ghost hunters have also had incredible luck capturing spirits in photographs taken with digital cameras, or even snapped with cell phones. IR and full-spectrum cameras are fantastic tools for groups that can afford them. But lots of people have gotten lots of amazing pictures with nothing more than a cell phone and a hunch.

I should probably mention here that there is a stunningly wonderful photograph of a nurse in one of the windows of the Bowen Building. The picture was taken on November 11, 2008, at one of the first fundraisers for the Save The Bowen Foundation. The group had brought a band in as entertainment. During a break, one of the band members was walking around the building. He pointed his camera at the second floor window at one end of the building, and snapped a picture. The photograph shows a beautiful young nurse, with long dark hair swept up into a loose Gibson Girl bun, wearing a nurse's crisp white uniform blouse.

Is it real?

A ghost picture this clear and defined is bound to create controversy. Some people point to the picture as evidence – a nurse standing in the window of the Bowen, how perfect! Others feel it's just too good to be true. Here are the facts. You can decide for yourself. (Photograph courtesy of Trent Jeffries; used by permission of Richard Weiss and Arlene Parr.)

The windowsills in that room are low; they reach to mid-thigh on a woman of average height. Perhaps the ghost is sitting in a chair next to the window...

But here's the thing: look closely at the corners of the window above that one, the window on the third floor. The metal edging of the window frame is formed by sharp right angles.

The upper corners of the second-floor window in the nurse photograph are rounded.

Does this mean the picture is faked? The guy who took it swears that it's real. He let his five year old son take it to school for show and tell. Sending it to the people in charge of promoting the Bowen's restoration is one thing. Would he have 'fessed up to a classroom full of first graders if the picture was a hoax?

That's something I'll let you decide on your own.

*EVPs – Voices From the Beyond*

As a paranormal investigator, I find EVPs, or electronic voice phenomena recordings, to be one of the most exciting ways of capturing evidence from the spirit world. The picture of an orb could just as easily be a piece of dust on a camera lens. That spooky shadow could have a perfectly rational explanation. Ah, but when you hear a voice speaking to you, a voice that you didn't hear when you were conducting the investigation, a voice that answers a specific question that you asked – that's when the hair on the back of your neck prickles, and a crazy, "I can't believe I'm hearing this" grin does a home-run slide onto your face.

Usually, during an investigation, you ask questions, then wait, to give the spirits a chance to answer. It's like a one-sided conversation, and sometimes it can be frustrating – and deathly boring. You tell yourself to be patient, that maybe, just maybe, you'll get your answers when you listen to the recording later.

The thing to remember is that the person you're talking to is dead. It's not like talking with the living. It's not even like conversing with the deceased in *Star Wars*, where the spirit is just a shimmery blue version of their old self, ready and willing to have a conversation with you. You've got an awful wide gulf to bridge, the distance between life and death.

The other thing to remember is that spirits seem to have a very fluid concept of time. From trying to have conversations with spirits, investigators have come to the conclusion that time has a very different meaning for the dead. The dead really don't care what time it is. And it doesn't seem to be important to them to answer questions right after they're asked, either. Talking with the dead does demand a certain amount of patience.

## Other Equipment

There are all sorts of fun toys that ghost hunters can play with. On one of my first visits to the Pollak Hospital, in December 2011, the members of Illinois Ghost Seekers Society showed me quite a few of them.

A lot of this equipment is designed to either give off or measure electromagnetic energy. The theory is pretty simple, as far as ghost hunting goes – the human body is basically a great big battery. The essence, the spark we call "life", can be described as electricity. (Just picture Dr. Frankenstein trying to harness lightning to animate his Creature.) One of the first steps in any investigation is to do a walkthrough with an EMF (electromagnetic frequency) meter, or a K-II meter (same thing, but with lights instead of a numbered gauge). The investigators trace power sources such as electrical conduits and large appliances, identifying them and eliminating them as sources of false readings on the meters.

So, the theory goes, if electromagnetic energy equals a spark of life, maybe it also signals the presence of a ghostly entity. That's why so much of this equipment focuses on energy – either measuring it, or giving it off so that the spirits in the area can use it to manifest more strongly.

Krystal Depew, of IGSS, showed me a device called an EPod that measures static electricity. It's a small cylinder made of white plastic, with three lights – red, blue, green – in order of sensitivity. When there's activity around, the red light will come on, then the blue light might join it. If the green light flickers on as well, something's happening. The whole thing looks much like the children's electronic game Simon Says.

In the Men's Ward, where there's usually quite a lot of activity, Krystal set up a device called a Rempod. Again, this involves electromagnetic energy. The Rempod actually puts out an electromagnetic field. It's a black cylinder, on which sits a white plastic top with four plastic posts. When the EM field is broken – or when some entity comes close enough to suck up some energy from the field the Rempod is emitting – the posts light up, green-red-blue-yellow, and the whole device glows and makes this weird sci-fi sound.

In the main hallway, one of the IGSS investigators set up an EM pump next to a child's ball. The EM pump emits electromagnetic energy in spurts, high then low. Again, the source of energy is meant to lure entities closer, giving them the strength to manifest or to affect their environment. Once, Krystal told me, the ball rolled all the way down the hallway. Did some child spirits suck enough energy from the EM pump to be able to play with the ball?

Some investigators feel that EVPs, or ghost voices, are not only aural experiences. They theorize that EVPs can be the result not only of sound waves, but also of EMF surges. So an EM pump could also, theoretically, give the spirits more material with which to cobble together EVPs.

Krystal showed me several other fun toys – the SEM, that measures electromagnetic energy, static electricity, and the level of ions in the air. Any change in any of those fields will make the alarm sound with a loud, high-pitched squeal. There was also a device cleverly called "Gotcha Ghosts", which turned out to be a K-II meter attached to a digital voice recorder. The neat trick with this machine was that it wouldn't record human voices – it would only pick up EVPs.

Some of these devices can serve double duty. For example, the K-II meter measures electromagnetic energy, and reveals it by lighting up a row of lights from green to red, depending on the strength of the EMF field. Investigators quite often use this tool for communication as well as detection. They invite the spirit to come closer – the closer the spirit energy gets to the meter, the more lights light up. They can also ask the spirit to answer questions this way. A colorful sweep of the lights, green to yellow to red, usually means "yes". (A dark meter either means "no", or it means there aren't any ghosts around and you're pretty much just talking to empty air.)

And all this stuff takes a while to set up – sometimes a *long* while. Lee Wagner, of Peoria Paranormal Society, told me that when they were setting up for an overnight investigation at the Pollak Hospital, one of the paying guests wandered over to him as he was laying some of the seven hundred feet of cable and cords that connect the cameras to the video feed in Command Central. The "civilian" asked, with thinly concealed impatience, "So when are you guys gonna be ready to start?"

"Right after the next commercial," was Lee's sardonic reply.

*The Personal Touch*

With all the fancy, high tech toys available to paranormal investigators these days, it's good for ghost hunters to remember that often, one's own senses can be useful tools as well. Just paying attention to your surroundings – what was that noise? Did that shadow just move? – can be valuable.

"I've been here so long, I can tell you which noises are raccoons in the walls and which are ghosts," Chris says of the Pollak Hospital. You don't have to be a sensitive, or a medium, to notice what's going on around you. Personal experience is much harder to quantify than, say, a reading of seven on an EMF meter, or an eighteen-degree drop on a thermometer. But using your own five senses – and sometimes even the sixth one – can be useful for ghost detection.

Chris spoke with a sensitive who experienced an inexplicable feel of anxiety during her visit to the asylum. The weather, which had been sunny, had changed, and the overcast sky was beginning to spit rain. "The patients were allowed to wander the hilltop, but whenever the weather changed like that and it started to rain, a bell would ring to call the inmates back to shelter. The ravines around the hilltop could be treacherous if they filled with water during a rainstorm. A patient could easily trip, fall into the ravine, and be swept away to drown," Chris explained. So a sudden rainstorm could provoke anxiety in a patient caught out unawares, and that's what the sensitive picked up.

You do have to know what it is you're experiencing, though. I was at the Pollak Hospital for an investigation in April 2012 when an investigator hurried up to me, eyes alight, panting with barely suppressed excitement.

"I was in the cemetery just outside, and I smelled perfume! I think it was a spirit trying to communicate with me!"

I mentally looked at the calendar, and my heart sank. "Did it smell like flower-scented bubble gum?"

The investigator stared at me in wonder. *How did she KNOW that?* "Yeah, yeah it did!"

"I hate to tell you this" – and I really truly did – "but that wasn't the sign of a ghostly presence, not this time. It's mid-April. The black locust is in bloom. That's what you were smelling." The ghost hunter's face fell, but unfortunately, debunking experiences is an important part of paranormal investigation. It's important because, when you've eliminated every possible rational explanation for the unexplained, what's left just might turn out to be evidence. In this case, though, the supernatural was merely natural.

I happened to be present for another debunking, during GUARD's investigation of Stone Country in December 2009. The dance floor of the former gymnasium is a wide-open space. Investigators had set up a camera in one corner to record the entire room. The camera captured what looked like intermittent flashes of light up in the corner of the ceiling. First a white light would blink on, then slowly fade. Then, in the same spot, there would be a flash of color: red, green, blue. GUARD's evidence analysis team spent quite some time examining those mysterious flashes of light. Their conclusion?

There was a shiny Mylar balloon up near the ceiling that had escaped from a party the week before. It had drifted up to a quiet corner and was sitting there, rotating just enough in any slight breeze to catch the light and throw it back in a tantalizing flash of silver and brilliant color.

*"Christopher"*

The thing to remember is that even with all the fun toys investigators have to play with, oftentimes your own senses will tell you just as much about what's going on around you. It won't be as scientific, and it will be much more subjective, but it can also be much more personal. All you have to do is open yourself up to the possibility of the unknown.

One of my very best experiences with the supernatural happened in the basement of the Pollak Hospital. This was in April 2012 (when the black locust was in bloom). Peoria Paranormal was hosting an overnight investigation. I had ridden my Ducati Monster from Pekin to Bartonville, so I had a nice heavy motorcycle jacket to wear in the unheated building.

Stacy and I had come out of the office to look for the other investigators. Someone told us that there was a group in the basement with Derek, who was using a ghost box. As you'll see later in this chapter, there is something in the basement that really doesn't like Derek. Hanging out with Derek in the basement of the Pollak with a ghost box is a near-guarantee of Fun Times. So we hurried down the stairs to join the group.

I was still wearing my jacket, but my hands were bare. The chill in the basement was noticeable, but I've never let a bit of cold bother me, especially on a ghost hunt. Sometimes, it's just part of the experience. We were standing around in a circle, about six or seven of us, with the ghost box sitting on the floor in the center of the circle. The ghost box was giving us plenty of action, and fortunately, the nasty spirit seemed to be lying low for the moment. The conversation coming out of the box was cordial. We asked, "How many spirits are here with us?"

"*Ten.*" Moments later, a different voice confirmed, "*Yup – ten.*"

I was holding my notebook, with my recorder flat on top of it (to reduce moving-around noise), in my right hand, and I wasn't paying much attention to my left hand.

All of a sudden, I started noticing a feeling of warmth in my left hand. Remember, the building was chilly, but I was wearing my jacket, so I wasn't cold enough to be uncomfortable. But the feeling of warmth was evident. It was kind of tentative at first, but very soon, my left hand felt noticeably warm. The feeling of warmth never reached my palm; it was just on my fingers. It felt like I was holding my hand out to a comfortably crackling campfire, a pleasant sensation of soothing warmth. Stacy was on the other side of the group, and I called her over urgently, hoping she could tell me what was going on.

Someone asked, "Is it the little girl?" They meant Elizabeth, whom you'll meet later in the book.

"No," Stacy said, "It's a man. Sylvia, you have a fan!" The ghost box yelped "*Yes!*", and I grinned in delight.

Two people put EMF meters near my left hand as I stood there, holding very still. Both of the meters were pegging up into the red.

Someone else jokingly said, "This guy just wants to be in the book, that's all."

Stacy concentrated for a moment. Then she replied, "Actually, that's exactly what he wants."

My hand continued to feel pleasantly warm. At one time, I could feel several pulses of energy thrum through my fingers, as though someone were giving them a gentle squeeze. We asked, "Can you tell us your name?" The ghost box replied "*Christopher*". I smiled.

"Christopher. Of course I'll put you in the book. I promise."

After several minutes, the warmth faded. I was sorry to feel it go. I've said it before, I'm a skeptic by nature. I want to *see* the evidence, or hear it, or experience it for myself. After those few long minutes in the basement, I could say, to my own satisfaction, that I'd had a genuine paranormal experience. My first experience of being touched by a spirit was not the least bit frightening. It was brilliant, and I really hope it happens again sometime.

Several months later, I was visiting the Pollak again, this time in July. Merilee Mitchell was there, and Chris and I took her into the basement. Merilee is a talented sensitive, and she was able to tell us that Christopher was there with us again. Merilee described him as a young man, dark-haired, handsome. She said, "He likes you – not in a romantic way. He recognizes you, and he feels comfortable around you." I held my left hand out, inviting him to take it again, but all I felt that time was a slight tingle of heat and energy in my upturned palm.

# GHOST HUNTERS

*Rob Conover*

It was a sunny day in July when I parked in front of Rob Conover's house. Hardly an atmosphere to get the imagination primed to see spooks around every dark corner. But that's exactly what Rob does. On my way up to the front door of the cozy suburban home, I passed Rob's gray KIA in the driveway.

The vanity plate reads "I C DDPPL".

Rob led me into the front room of the house, the room that serves as the office for his paranormal investigation business. And it's big business. Conover is one of the most well-known names in the area when it comes to ghostbusting. The walls of the office are covered with framed newspaper articles and magazine covers that attest to Rob's years in the field.

"As of Friday a week ago, I've done 824 cases," Rob said with a note of pride in his voice.

Rob was a private detective in 1992 when he met the late Greta Alexander. Greta was a renowned psychic, a local legend who lived in nearby Delavan, Illinois. During their conversation, Greta told Rob that soon, he would begin investigating the paranormal.

"And you'll be doing this for the rest of your life," Greta said, with the certainty of the practiced seer.

"You are fulla shit," Rob told her.

Greta laughed in delight. "No one's ever said that to me before!"

Greta's prediction came true. Rob suffered a catastrophic accident, resulting in the loss of one of his fingers. This injury seemed to trigger a latent ability in him, expanding his perceptions of this world ... and the next. Rob developed a sixth sense, an ability to communicate with the spirits of the dead.

Rob Conover has been investigating haunted places for the past two decades, and now he can't imagine doing anything else. He has been out to Bartonville countless times. He shares a love of the Bowen Building with her owner, Richard Weiss, and her many other fans.

When October rolls around every year, local news outlets call Rob, knowing that his name gets attention in ghost hunting circles. Rob has worked with many television and radio stations, leading hapless reporters and camera crews on a wild ride through the haunted places of central Illinois. He loves taking reporters to the asylum in Bartonville: he knows they'll come away with a great story to share.

For a Halloween story in 1998, Rob took a reporter from the *Peoria Journal Star* into the Bowen Building, which at that time was owned by Wes Durand. Rob and Valerie Lilley, the reporter, both had new flashlights for their excursion into the building.

"We got in there, and both of our brand new flashlights went out at the same time," Rob told me. "All at once, it was refrigerator dark in there. Valerie lets out this fire engine whoop ..." Rob shook his head, remembering.

According to Rob, there were two spirits in the Bowen Building named "Ed" and "Al". "They were old buddies of mine. I could always rely on them to scare whoever I took in there." Ed and Al showed up for Valerie's visit to the Bowen. As Rob and Valerie made their way through the dark halls, Rob's "old buddies" manifested as a cloud of glowing blue ectoplasm in the middle of a hallway.

"You can't write that," Valerie's editor snapped when she told him about her experience.

"Why not? That's what happened!" she shot back.

The editor snorted. "It was probably rigged." To prove his point, the editor snuck into the Bowen a few nights later, along with a junior editor. Valerie went with the two men. The three of them crept into the building at one in the morning. Whatever they saw in there scared them so badly that shortly afterwards, they came screaming out of the building. The editor dropped his new leather jacket in his hurry to escape. Beside him, Valerie panted, "Hey, did you know? You dropped your jacket."

"Fuck my jacket," the skeptical editor wheezed. "I'm leaving!"

Ed and Al no longer haunt the Bowen. According to Rob, he has released twenty-eight spirits from the building, including his "old buddies". Rob told me that he got rid of Ed first, but Al was tougher to release. Rob finally cornered Al on the third floor, in front of a television crew, as it turned out.

Rob's Christian faith has served him well in his career as a "ghost buster". His faith seems to carry him through situations that make other ghost hunters quiver with fear. Rob got a call at ten o'clock one night from one of the Bowen volunteers, a self-styled "demon expert".

"We need you down here," the volunteer insisted. "Everyone's been run out of the basement. There's something horrible down there!"

Rob made the short drive from Pekin to Bartonville. As he came up Pfeiffer Road to the Bowen, he saw a group of people standing outside on the lawn. None of them looked very eager to go back inside the building.

Rob parked his car and heaved his bulk out of the driver's seat. "I'll go check things out," he announced to the huddled knot of frightened people.

"You're going by yourself?" It was J. C., the guy who had made the panicked phone call.

"Well, someone's got to do it, Mr. Demonologist," Rob drawled.

In the end, Rob didn't go alone. He took Bill Russell and Bill's infrared camera with him. The two men went cautiously down to the basement. At the bottom of the stairs, they turned to the right.

Suddenly a black mass came boiling out of the tunnel at the end of the basement hallway. A pair of red eyes burned at head-height, fixing the two men with a menacing glare. Rob held up the Bible that is his constant companion. The ruddy glare of the burning eyes glinted off the gold leaf on the edge of the Good Book.

"In that instant, the black mass just disappeared," Rob told me. "We felt the entire atmosphere change. Everything got lighter, more relaxed. It was the gold leaf on the Bible that did it."

With all the experiences he's had at the Peoria State Hospital, it's no wonder the asylum holds a special place in Rob's heart. On July 7. 2012, Rob Conover and his wife, Alesia, renewed their wedding vows in a short ceremony, which was held on the front lawn of the Bowen Building. Rob, Alesia, and the minister stood on the stone porch of the building, only steps away from the door leading into the blackness of the basement.

## *Central Illinois Ghost Hunters (CIGH)*

Members of Central Ilinois Ghost Hunters also shared several stories with me. I met with Linda Hambrick and Beth McCabe, who have both encountered spirits in the cemeteries around the asylum grounds.

In Cemetery 3, someone kept turning off the instant-read thermometer as the group was investigating. Linda finally gave up on keeping the thermometer on. An EVP captured at the time reveals the giggles of what Linda describes as a "childlike lady". It was also at Cemetery 3 that members of the group saw a dark figure walking along the road – a figure that suddenly disappeared as they watched.

The group was investigating outside the Bowen, at the corner of the building next to Constitution Drive. Their digital voice recorders, sitting in the window leading to the basement, picked up a man's deep voice chillingly saying *"Die"*. Another EVP captured a woman's voice, curious, asking, *"Good <u>night</u> – who is that?"*

The group had a very intriguing experience while investigating one of the smaller buildings at the asylum. Two female members of the team were walking around outside the building, taking pictures and letting their voice recorders run. They had walkie-talkies with them, but the walkies were off. One of the investigators turned to the other and said, "Well, I guess it's time to go."

Without being keyed, the walkie-talkie blurted out a staticky burp of sound. The words were unintelligible, but the voice was human. The investigators turned to each other, open-mouthed.

"What? Did you say 'hello'?" they asked the entity on the other end of the walkie.

The walkie-talkie crackled again, and this time the voice came through a little more clearly. *"I said, that's a wrap."*

Another time, the group caught a very clear EVP of a woman's voice asking in a querulous whisper, *"What the hell was that?"*

In contrast to many paranormal investigation groups, CIGH offers a value-added service along with their investigations. They, like Rob Conover, have the experience and the willingness to send spirits into the Light. Linda will only do this if the spirit wishes to go, and if the client wants it too. (If a client, or another family member, is frightened by the presence of a spirit, Linda will encourage the spirit to move on.)

Linda and Beth agreed that sometimes, people go to Bartonville in search of a thrill, or simply out of curiosity. That's when they end up bringing something home with them. "I can't tell you how many calls I've gotten, where someone's been having problems, things moving around in the house, and they'll say, 'Well, I *did* go to Bartonville last weekend.' One woman told us her cat was cowering behind the washing machine, too unnerved by something to come out of there for more than a few minutes at a time. People don't realize, you *can* have something follow you home."

The group did thirteen investigations one October a few years ago. At least seven of those investigations, Linda told me, had their origins at the Peoria State Hospital.

*Dianne*

One of the many fascinating people I met in the course of writing this book was a talented medium who asked me to use only her first name. Dianne is an intense woman with long dark hair. The fine lines around her eyes seem to give testament to the sights she's seen.

"My mom warned me when I was a kid, 'Don't tell anyone you can do this.' I think she figured it would make my life miserable if people knew I had the ability to see things they couldn't."

It hasn't made her miserable, but it's certainly made her life interesting. Dianne has made many visits to the asylum in Bartonville. She sees the place a little differently than everyone else does. Dianne described her visit to the Bowen Building. I listened, entranced.

Her visions started even before she went into the building. She was standing at the side of the Bowen next to Pfeiffer Road, looking up at the windows. "I saw a make patient wearing a hospital gown. He was just looking out of the window. He seemed medicated, almost catatonic. He wasn't doing anything, just staring."

Dianne's ability told her that long before the Bowen was built, the land on which it now stands was rich farmland. She saw a farmer "just hanging out" on the front lawn of the Bowen.

"At one point, the Bowen was used as a dormitory." I nodded; this was familiar to me from my research. "When I went inside, I could see beds in the rooms, and I could see people lying in the beds."

Anne Pritchard of Mid America Ghost Hunters led the tour that day. As they passed a specific point in the hallway, Dianne spoke up. "This was the nurses' station. I can see nurses going in and out of the door." Anne confirmed this for her.

As fascinating as it must be to see into the past, Dianne does find this ability distressing at times. She not only sees people going about their daily lives, she can hear them and speak with them as well. And sometimes, their stories are tragic. Near the nurses' station, Dianne saw a lady who looked lost and frightened. "Why do you stay here?" Dianne asked her.

The spirit's reply was simple. *"Because I don't know anywhere else to go."*

(On a different visit, Dianne met a spirit in Cemetery 2, where Bookbinder is buried. The spirit, a younger woman, seemed very depressed. She kept saying, *"I shouldn't be here."*)

Dianne's experiences in the hallways of the Bowen Building were similar to those of other mediums who have visited the place. She felt uncomfortable in exactly the same places in the basement that gave Rob Conover the willies. Because of her heightened sensitivity, she has had much closer brushes with the spirits of the Bowen than most of us will ever experience.

Perhaps understandably, Dianne's not keen on being touched. "It's a gut reaction," she told me. Of course, when a spirit suddenly materialized *right* in front of her as she was walking down a hallway, her first reaction was naturally to yelp, "DO NOT TOUCH ME!"

She explained it to me in terms she figured I could understand. "When a spirit really wants to get your attention, it feels like something's invading your personal space, but even more than that. It feels like it's inside you; it can affect your moods, if you let it."

Dianne comes from a tradition of Native American culture, both by descent and through her own spirituality. She uses a sage smudge, burning dried sage and wafting the smoke around her body with a feather fan, when the spirit world gets a little too pushy in its demands for her attention.

Of course, she sometimes resorts to simply telling the spirits, "Stop following me!"

*Living Dead Paranormal*

If you visit Rocky Fourman's website, the home page for Living Dead Paranormal, you will see a group picture on the intro page. Four big guys in black shirts and baseball caps stand in a formidable line, arms crossed, faces serious. These no-nonsense ghost hunters are Living Dead Paranormal, and in the spring of 2012 they came from Ohio to investigate the Pollak Hospital.

They documented their experiences in a film called The Asylum Project, which can be found on their website, http://livingdeadparanormal.blogspot.com. The half-hour film includes interviews with Stacy Carroll and Chris Morris, interspersed with the crew's experiences at the Pollak Hospital. Derek Waldschmidt of Peoria Paranormal Society was interviewed briefly for the film, and he shared his opinion that the Pollak is one of the most haunted buildings on the hilltop.

The ghosts at the hospital must have been feeling especially frisky that night. They decided, apparently, to pull out all the stops and give the Living Dead crew an evening of real scares.

As the crew was interviewing Chris, thumps and bangs could be heard in the background. Chris grinned, recognizing the ghost they call "Heavy Boots" making his presence known. She told the interviewer about a set of double doors in the Men's Death Ward that will swing open on its own – even when it's securely locked.

"We checked the doors during the haunted house last October," Chris said. "There were so many people wandering around for the haunt, and we didn't want people coming in through that entrance, so we made sure the doors were closed securely and locked. There were several high school kids, volunteers, working in that room of the haunt, when those locked doors swung open about three feet. Scared the crap out of those poor kids!"

During the actual investigation, the crew was in the Men's Ward when they heard a shriek come from the main hallway. It sounded, to them, like a woman's scream. The ghost hunters followed the sound out into the hallway. As they stood in the hallway outside the Men's Ward, something flew up from the basement and screamed in their faces. The camera tilted crazily as the ghost hunters flailed and beat at the unseen attacker. The camera's sound recorder caught a child's laughter as the men yelled in startled fear.

Realizing that the screaming entity had come up from the basement, the crew went down the stairs and went all the way back to the morgue. Josh Fourman, the lead investigator, commented several times, "It's colder than shit back here." The guys figured out that the groaning scream they'd heard originally, that they thought had come from the main hallway, was actually the sound of the heavy freezer door slamming shut … in the empty morgue.

All evening, the group was treated to knocks, bangs, and screams. The climax of the evening came very late that night, after the investigation was over. The four ghost hunters had set up cots in the tour room, the room just inside the front hallway of the building. After a night of excitement, the men wanted to get a few hours' sleep before their drive home to Ohio.

All four men were sound asleep at about three o'clock in the morning, when something lifted two of their cots about a foot in the air, then dropped them back down with a crash. The ghost hunters all came shrieking out of the building, nearly running into the group of volunteers that was still standing outside the building chatting.

Chris, Stacy, Jill, Jeff, and Jackie were still out in the darkness, talking quietly. There's something about the Pollak Hospital that draws the people who love it to stay as long as they possibly can. I've felt this pull myself – it's a feeling of peace and safety that just makes you want to stay there.

Chris and the others were sitting around in front of the building, talking quietly and enjoying the spring evening, when the front door slammed open and four ghost hunters, their clothes rumpled with sleep and their eyes wide with terror, came tumbling out of the building and down the concrete steps. Hearts racing with adrenaline, they gasped out what had happened to them.

Stacy, Chris, and the others shared knowing glances and grins. The ghosts at the Pollak Hospital aren't shy about entertaining themselves, that's for sure.

Later, I spoke with Greg, one of the investigators. His version differed just slightly from the story Chris had told me. Greg said that the guys had set up their cots in the hallway, head to head. The four were sound asleep when Rocky and Shaun felt something. Rocky woke up just enough to mumble, "Something moved." Shaun groggily said, "Shut up and go back to sleep."

Luckily, the Fourman brothers had had the presence of mind to set up a night vision camera to film the hallway as they slept. Shaun was reviewing the tape when he saw his and Rocky's cots lift, then slam back down. Very calmly, he paused the tape and went outside to smoke a cigarette. Only then did he come back and press PLAY. "I couldn't watch it," he told me.

Greg's version of their exit from the Pollak Hospital is just a bit different than Chris's version, too.

"We weren't running," Greg claimed, "but we weren't dragging our feet, either."

*Pollak Investigation, February 4, 2012*

I've been to the Pollak Hospital many times, and every time, I've come away with a story. One of my most memorable visits came in February, 2012.

Like I said in the introduction to this book, I go into haunted places so my readers don't have to. The rest of this chapter on Ghost Hunters is a rundown of one evening's investigation. The group I was working with that night was Peoria Paranormal Society. It was my first experience with using a ghost box, which I found utterly fascinating. You'll get to use it too. You get to come with us into the darkened hallways of the Pollak Hospital. I'll take you through the evening, and I'll be sure to point out the really cool parts along the way. Also, you can listen to some of the audio we captured that night at the Fractured Spirits fan page on Facebook.

Ready?

I spent most of the evening with Derek Waldschmidt, one of Peoria Paranormal's investigators, and Stacy, the Pollak's resident sensitive. Peoria Paranormal was hosting an overnight investigation in the hospital, and the building was humming with activity. Investigators were taking groups of newbies out from Command Central into different areas of the hospital. We headed to the basement first, only to find that a group of people was already down there working. We decided to go back upstairs, as we've discovered that there's a correlation between the number of people down in the basement, and the amount of activity they can experience. Having too many people down there at once seems to overpower the spirits, and they get shy.

We went up the stairs, our flashlight beams stabbing at the darkness. I've gotten better about walking around a place in the dark (or the near-dark), as long as there are people around me. But I still don't like to be the last in a group, especially going up stairs. As we trotted up the concrete stairs, Stacy oh-so-casually mentioned that there was someone following us up the stairs. I thought to myself, "Well, duh." I *knew* I had arranged it so I wasn't the last one up. I *knew* there was someone behind me. When I got to the top of the steps, I turned and held the door for the ghost hunter I was honestly convinced was the last one of our group up the stairs.

There was no one behind me.

Shaking off the sudden chill that cramped in my lower belly, I followed the group into the Women's Ward. Derek explained the EMF meter to our little band, many of whom had never done any investigation before this evening.

"We had a little girl running back and forth last time, and it would blip every time she ran past."

Stacy spoke up. "I just wanted to let you know, they like you talking about them. They think it's cool." She shrugged.

Derek turned the ghost box on. The ghost box, also affectionately known as a "Shack Hack" (because everything you need to make one can be found at Radio Shack), is a deeply interesting tool for paranormal investigation. The theory behind it is simple: the radio scans constantly through the AM dial, providing a continuous stream of white noise. Sometimes, snippets of what the deejays are saying sneak through as well. The spirits, apparently, are able to use these blurts of sound to speak, usually to answer questions.

Sometimes, as Derek has discovered more than once, the spirits can use these radio waves to form words that you will never hear on the AM stations. As Stacy points out, "If someone was a jerk while they were alive, they're gonna be obnoxious when they're dead. Some spirits are just assholes."

The radio chattered softly as it scanned through the AM band. Snippets of sound laced the air, and we listened, trying to pick out something coherent from the quick rhythmic mutterings.

"Can you tell us how many spirits are here?"

At first we picked out *"ten"* from the gibberish that flipped past. We asked again.

"Can you tell us how many spirits are here?"

This time, *"nine"* and *"hundred"* flashed past.

Sounds came in a fast-paced rhythm from the ghost box. Sometimes there were snippets of actual words, or flashes of music. For the inexperienced, it was hard at times to pinpoint what the box was trying to say. Derek tried a different question.

"Can you tell me what my name is?"

About ten seconds later, a radio deejay said, "DEREK".

It's always good manners to thank the spirits for interacting with you, especially if they're answering questions. After we heard Derek's name come out of the box so clearly, I spoke out loud to the room, thanking the ghosts for their cooperation. As I spoke, I wasn't paying attention to the constant stream of sound coming out of the ghost box, but Derek and Stacy are both old pros at it.

"Oop – I heard the B-word," Derek said.

Stacy nodded. "Yep."

"What, B-I-T-C-H?" I asked.

Derek nodded in the darkness. "Yeah. This scans the AM dial, so there's no reason to hear bad language, ever. But sometimes the ghosts like to cuss. We've heard the B-word, we've heard F-bombs …"

I was miffed. I spoke aloud, "So I tell you guys how smart you are to use this to talk to us, and you call me a bitch?"

The ghost box hesitated, then threw out, "*I guess not.*"

Someone seemed to be in a mood, though. Derek asked, "Are you okay with us being here?"

"*Leave.*"

"Do you want me to leave the Women's Ward because I'm male?" Derek pressed.

"*Leave,*" the box spat. The forceful voice did sound female.

"You don't really want me to leave, do you?"

"*Leave.*"

Derek pushed harder. "I'm not gonna leave, I'm gonna walk around and –"

"*Leave!*"

"You've got two different women here," Stacy observed.

I chimed in, trying to defuse the tension. "Do you like being able to use the radio to communicate?"

"*Yes.*"

Then a man's voice came out of the radio. "*Leave immediately.*"

"Do you want us to go?"

"*Yeah.*"

"Can we come back later?" I asked.

"*Yeah.*"

We left the Women's Ward. Four of us, Derek, Stacy, myself, and an investigator named Jo, went down the hallway, past the basement door, into one of the patient exam rooms. The door between this room and the adjoining one was still painted a pleasing orchid-lavender shade – a remnant of Dr. Zeller's use of color therapy to calm unruly patients. In this room, we watched the EMF meter fluctuate between the green and yellow lights, indicating a strong EMF field – a ghost? – as Jo reported that she felt someone playing with her hair.

As we left the room, Stacy said, "There's a spirit that likes this room. He'll peek out of this room when we leave. We call him 'Mr. Peekaboo'. You'll be able to see him if you look back down the hallway."

"There was a blip on the EMF meter when you said that," Derek said with a grin.

As soon as we sat down in the Men's Ward, the temperature in the room seemed to plummet, and Derek began coughing violently – racking, spasming coughs. Between breaths, he gasped, "It feels like someone's *making* me cough, like I'm supposed to be a patient here."

We set the EMF meter next to the ghost box on a chair – the one next to mine, as it happened. The meter blipped up into the yellow, and Derek said, "Looks like someone just sat down by Sylvia."

"Hello! How are you tonight?" I asked.

The ghost box spoke immediately. *"Good."*

"Glad to hear it!" And I really was!

Working with a ghost box is a heady experience. Sounds flip past incredibly quickly, at a steady pulse, of, say, four snippets of sound per second. Sometimes bursts of speech or music leap into the air. Underlying all of this random noise is a constant electronic hum – a rough middle C, ragged at the edges, not a pure tone.

As in EVP recording, when you ask a question, sometimes it takes a while to get an answer out of the ghost box. At other times, the answer is blurted out immediately. Most of the time, the radio is spitting out indistinct blats of sound. Stacy and Derek, having worked with the ghost box so often, are adept at identifying words as they flash past. Sometimes, it took me several passes listening to the recordings at home before I caught what they had heard straight away during the investigation. But sometimes, the words are unmistakably clear, even to someone unused to the device.

Ten of us huddled in a circle in the basement, looking down at the cluster of equipment on the floor. I'd put my digital voice recorder down between the two EMF meters. The ghost box chirruped constantly to itself. We were in the basement room closest to the stairs. An open doorway led into another, slightly smaller room. When the Pollak Hospital was open, the farther room was used as the morgue, where bodies waited for burial in one of the asylum cemeteries or to be claimed by family. In the morgue there is a small storage area about the size of a walk-in freezer. This tiny annex has a huge, heavy, solid metal door. Volunteers at the hospital say they can hear the groan and slam of that heavy door all the way upstairs … even when no one is in the basement.

"Elizabeth", the little girl who haunts the basement, was out playing with her visitors that night. When we came down to join the group, the investigators who were already down there said they'd seen the shadow of a little girl. A short, solid black figure would peek through the doorway into the morgue, then draw back. Annette, an investigator, told me, "We could see her head and the outline of her body in the doorway."

We turned the ghost box on. The first word it spat out was *"sick"*. The EMF meters were constantly spiking up into the yellow and red lights. The air in the basement fairly pulsed with the energy of the spirits swirling around us.

Derek soon locked horns with one of the entities in the basement. Derek and "Seth" have crossed paths before, and "Seth" doesn't like Derek at all.

"Are you mad that I'm back down here again?"

An irritated, sulky silence from the box.

"What's your name?" an investigator asked.

*"I'm mad,"* the box snarled.

"Who are you mad at?"

*"Derek."*

"Do you want me to leave? Do you want me to get out of here?" Derek asked.

*"No."*

"Are you scared of us right now?"

*"No."* The answer was immediate, right on the heels of Derek's question.

The ghost box was still scanning furiously through the AM band. "How many living people are down here?" Derek asked. There was a long pause as the box scanned.

"*Ten.*"

"That's very good," Derek said. "How many people are down here with us that have died?"

"*Twelve.*"

Tony, another investigator, spoke up. "This EMF meter is bouncing on ten. I'm getting a pretty good spike over here. You can't get a spike like that unless you bring it over to the 220 coming from the city. Engineering-wise, this should not be happening. Realistically, this should not be happening." Tony's voice was calm, but there was an undercurrent of tense excitement swirling underneath his words.

Stacy spoke. "Elizabeth, are you here?"

"Right now, I think the little girl's here and the other guy's gone," Tony said.

"Yes, she's right here," Stacy said. As the sensitive of the group, she had the best handle on which spirit's energy was present at any one time. "This is her energy. Can you come back, light 'em up for us?"

One after another, in a rhythmic pattern, the lights on the meters in the investigators' hands leapt from green to yellow, up into the red, then back down.

"She likes to do that," Stacy said, fondness softening her usual no-nonsense tone. "She likes to go from one to the other. She's very quick. She can hit all those meters – she likes the lights."

"Elizabeth, when I get to how old you are, can you light up the lights for us?" Stacy paused. "Are you four years old? Are you five? Are you six?" The meters spiked into the red at "five", then fell back to the green. There was no response to "six".

Stacy repeated the question. "Can you tell us how old you are again?"

There was a spit of sound from the ghost box. "*You know.*"

Derek spoke up. "Yes, I know that you're five, I just want to hear you say it."

The ghost box whined, "*Okay ...*"

Then a male voice snapped, "*Back up,*" and that's when things really started to get interesting. My meter jumped to eight. Derek muttered, "I think my buddy's coming back." Stacy, the sensitive, looked up from her meter and said, "Be careful, guys – it's gonna get wild."

"Whoa, did you hear that deep voice?" Derek said. "What's your name, buddy? The big guy?"

There was no answer from the ghost box.

"Do you want me to leave?"

"*Buzz off,*" the box snapped.

"Do you want me to leave, so I can be by myself in the hallway?" Derek pressed. "So you can follow me?"

"*Maybe.*"

Someone else asked, "Do you want him to go into the other room, with the freezer?"

A deep "*YES*" from the box.

"Challenge accepted," Derek said flatly.

We pressed Derek with questions – do you want a flashlight? Do you want someone to go in there with you? Tony asked the ghost box, "Do you want anybody to go with Derek?"

"*No.*"

Derek asked, "Do you want me to go all by myself?"

"*Pussy,*" the box spat.

"It wants to get you by yourself," Tony realized.

"Can you push me in the chest like you did last time?" Derek challenged.

*"Doubt it,"* the box replied in a sulky snarl.

"Why can't you, are you getting too weak?"

There was no answer from the box.

Tony spoke next. "Are you afraid of Derek?"

The box scanned the dial for a few long moments. Then a deep voice rolled out of the box.

*"Never."*

"Do you think Derek's afraid of you?"

There was a long pause, while the box scanned. Then the deep voice spoke again.

*"Doesn't matter."*

Another investigator, Mindy, came downstairs at that point. We asked the spirits, "Is it okay if Mindy joins us?"

*"Works for me,"* the ghost box shrugged.

Then the K-II meters pegged up into the red and started beeping madly. All of the investigators shared nervous glances. What was going on here?

"Do you want Mindy to leave?"

Mindy spoke up. "Tell me to leave. I want to hear you tell me to get out."

A very faint *"nope"* blurted from the box.

Just then, we all heard a low rumble from the other room, the room that used to be the morgue. It was the unmistakable deep *creak-and-SLAM!* of the heavy door to the freezer slamming shut.

There was no one in the morgue.

"Are you back there, in the freezer?" Our voices were sharp with fear.

"*I locked it,*" came the taunting deep voice.

"Did you just shut the door to the freezer?"

Another, different voice spat out, "*Leave.*"

Again, we heard the low metallic rumbling scrape of the door. This time, there was no final slam.

"That was the door again," someone muttered.

I asked, "Will someone go and see what position the door is in now?" I paused. "'Cause I'm sure as shit not going."

That brought a rustle of nervous laughter. One of the guys went to the doorway, peeked through, and reported back: "It's open again."

"And it was closed before?"

"Yeah, it was closed."

I can't speak for anyone else, but I can still remember the sick chill that settled in the pit of my stomach when I wondered just *what* had slammed, then opened, that heavy metal freezer door.

Derek relented. "Do you want me to leave?"

"*What's the difference?*" the box sighed.

As we spoke with the ghost box, Mindy wandered around the dark basement taking photographs. We asked, "Do you like Mindy taking pictures?"

The ghost box snapped, "*You – go 'way.*"

"Are you angry at Mindy for taking pictures here?"

"*Yes.*"

Mindy said, "Sorry … I apologize."

"Do you accept Mindy's apology?"

There was no response from the ghost box. The silence went on for so long that I finally asked, "Are you still here with us?"

There was a sobbed *"No"*, then *"Yes."* We interpreted this to mean "No", the spirits didn't accept Mindy's apology, and "Yes", they were still present.

Mindy, still holding her camera, said, "Do ya want me to leave? … Tell me to leave."

There were several moments of silence from the ghost box. Then …

*"Yes … leave."*

"See ya," Mindy said, and scooted up the stairs. The rest of us huffed nervous laughter.

Derek tried once more. "Do you want me to go back to that freezer?"

Two different voices responded, *"No."*

"Do you want us to go back upstairs?"

A very faint *"yes"* came from the box.

"Do you want us all to go back upstairs?"

There was a long silence from the box. Then two different voices spoke.

*"Yes."*

*"He's right."*

I was absolutely, positively *not* the last one up the stairs that time.

As an investigator, I find the ghost box utterly and eternally fascinating. I am a hopeless, unrelenting skeptic. On the surface, I think the ghost box is a complete load of crap. However, I am also, deep in my heart, someone who very desperately wants to be convinced that ghosts do exist and can communicate with us from wherever they are. That part of me, the part that wants to believe, thinks the ghost box is the Coolest Toy Ever. Yeah, I'm conflicted that way.

I have absolutely no clue how the spirits can pick words out of radio waves. I don't *care* how they do it. It just thrills me that they *can* do it. When we're standing around asking questions, and the ghost box blurts out answers that *make sense* – man, that nearly beats EVPs in my book. This is a real, honest-to-God, real-time conversation happening, and it is flat-out thrilling.

And honestly, I think it's got to be pretty neat for the spirits, too. The lucky ones who have figured out how to use the ghost box to communicate – it must be a powerful charge for them. It may be a reminder of what it's like to carry on a conversation.

Maybe … maybe it's almost like being alive again.

# THE BOWEN BUILDING

*"That's an EVP that I would have put all over the world, if I could. I'd say, 'You have to listen to this,' because it was that clear."* -- *Kristy Carmody, a visitor to the Bowen Building*

It was late at night in November, and bitterly cold. The weather had been mild for fall, but it had changed that week, and now winter was here with a chill promise of things to come. I was at the abandoned, shuttered Bowen Building in Bartonville, along with several friends. We were there to hunt ghosts.

We all shivered in our heavy jackets as we gazed up at the darkly forbidding building. The Bowen Building, one of the last standing structures of the asylum, is constructed from large sand-colored blocks of stone. No glass remains in any of the windows, and the empty windows on the bottom floor are covered with weathered gray plywood boards. The whole building gives off a chill air of menace, even on the hottest days of summer. Here, at night with the breath of winter making us shiver through our coats and gloves, the building seemed alive with the unknown.

All of us crammed into a room on the first floor for the orientation. We sat on chilly metal chairs and stared around the room, taking in the peeling paint and the scrawls of spray painted graffiti. Shari checked the batteries in her video camera while I fidgeted. Our guides, Anne and Bob, gave us a quick rundown of the building's history. Bob, the guide who was to lead us through the building, shared his own experience with us.

"I was sitting in a chair in the hallway on the first floor, and I saw a dark, cloaked figure come out of one of the rooms. It stared at me for a second – not that it had eyes, but I *felt* it stare – then it glided back into the room. It looked like one of those things from the *Harry Potter* movies –"

"A Dementor?" I supplied.

"Yeah, a Dementor. It was black, and it moved like ... like it was made of smoke." Bob shuddered with the memory. "Scared me so bad I had to go outside for a while. Okay, fine, I didn't go back in 'til the next evening."

With that chilling image in our minds, we split up into two groups. Anne took one group and headed up to the attic, while our group went downstairs to the basement.

This happened to be my very first ghost tour, so I was on edge the whole time, not knowing what to expect. (Hey, every ghost hunter has to start somewhere.) When Bob told us that the morgue was in the basement, I felt a cold chill work its way down my spine. The morgue ... *brrrrr*.

When we were all gathered around the guide in the hallway next to the open door of the morgue, Bob told us we were going "lights out". This means turning off the flashlights. *All* of the flashlights. For someone like me, who nurses an irrational but life-long fear of the dark, this is like saying, "We're going to the aquarium – yay! And when we get to the shark exhibit, we're going to strip down to our skivvies and just hop right on in there with them, how's that sound?" I shivered and closed my eyes, seeking darkness on my own terms before the lights went out.

*Click.* The last flashlight was shut off, and we stood there, silent in the darkness. A strange sound came from somewhere down the hallway. I gasped, and nearly jumped out of my skin. "Are you okay?" the guide murmured.

"Yeah, fine," I muttered back. As we all stood there, listening hard in the utter blackness of the basement, I had heard a soft cooing moan, like the sobbing call of a pigeon, but without the trill. When we turned the flashlights back on, I apologized to the guide for startling, and explained the noise I'd heard.

"I heard it too," he said, his face serious.

We crowded through the narrow door into the morgue, our flashlights painting the walls with splashes of light. Once inside, we spread out, finding places along the walls. No one really wanted to stand in the middle of the room, where the drain was. That was too sharp of a reminder of what these walls had seen decades ago. Thankfully, Bob didn't suggest we turn the flashlights off. My nerves, wound nearly to the breaking point, surely would have snapped if I'd had to stand in a morgue in pitch-blackness.

We started to ask questions, hoping to catch some EVPs on the recorders whose red lights were scattered around the room. Shari looked down at her camera and frowned. She fiddled with a button. A few minutes later, she shook the camera, and mashed another button.

"This camera keeps turning itself off," she announced, her voice laced with irritation. "I've had to turn it back on like five times."

After leaving the morgue, we climbed the concrete stairs up to the attic. The narrow stairs were filthy with plaster dust. As with most of the building, the floor in the attic was too fragile to safely support the weight of dozens of people per night walking on it. So we were restricted to a small area at the top of the stairs. The rest of the attic was blocked off with waist-high sheets of plywood, giving us a clear view to the other end of the building.

We went lights-out again. "Watch closely," the guide whispered. He pointed across the large room, to the other end of the attic. "You're gonna see something really weird in a second." We looked out towards the other end of the attic. It was pitch black except for the soft glow of an EXIT sign. As we watched, the red glow of the sign faded into the blackness, then reappeared moments later, just exactly as if some dark phantom had crossed in front of it.

On the third floor, we encountered more strangeness. Again, the main part of the hallway was blocked off by plywood boards, so that we could see the debris-filled floor, but not walk on it. The dust lay thick on the floor, proving that no one had walked there for years. Our guide asked the familiar question: "Is there anyone here? If you're here, can you make a noise for us?"

From the middle of the hallway, up against the far wall, we all heard a quiet "*tap...tap...tap...tap...tap...tap...*" Then it stopped.

"Can you do that again for us, please?"

*Tap...tap...tap...tap...tap...tap...tap...*

Twice more, the mysterious taps repeated when we asked them to, seven or eight slow, measured taps at a time, then silence. We couldn't agree on what could be making the steady noise. Some people said it sounded like the ticking of a large grandfather clock. Other people swore it sounded like a steadily moving rocking chair, or like a child skipping rope. To me, it sounded like someone rapping a cane against the floor. Whatever made the noise, though, we all agreed that the tapping was meant to communicate with us.

As we made our way down another flight of stairs, I turned to a friend who, years before, had gone into the asylum after dark to explore. This was a favorite pastime for some adventurous teens, and the risk of getting caught by patrolling cops only added to the allure.

"So, when you guys were hanging out in here, crawling through tunnels and stuff, did you ever hear any weird noises?"

"All the time," came the calm reply. (This friend of mine is not easily flustered. Or spooked.)

"What did you do when you heard weird things? Did you ever think it was ghosts?"

My friend shrugged. "We always just assumed it was other kids out here making as much noise as we were. We just went the other way."


The Bowen Building is the iconic image of the Peoria State Hospital, and rightly so. Standing at the top of the hill on Pfeiffer Road, it is the building that is the most easily recognizable as one of the asylum buildings. Out of the sixty-five original cottages and hospitals, only thirteen structures remain. The Bowen is the one that looks like it has every right to be haunted.

The Bowen was, at one time, the public face of the Peoria State Hospital. (One could argue that it still is -- it graces the covers of several books about the asylum.) Wide porches stretched the length of the building, on the first and second floors. These porches wrapped around the building, and an additional porch connected the two arms of the U-shaped "back". What most people now consider the back of the building, the west side, was actually the front of the Bowen when it was in operation. This was where people who weren't affiliated with the hospital entered the building: visitors, or patients who hadn't yet been admitted. The "front" of the Bowen, the side closest to the Illinois River, was really the back. The wide porches at the back were a perfect place for nurses to step out for a breath of fresh air. Patients, too, were encouraged to stroll on the porches, and to watch whatever entertainment was taking place on the lawn – the "back yard". In spite of concerns for their safety, not one patient ever chose to do a swan dive off of the balconies. (For the rest of this chapter, for the sake of simplicity, I'll use the wording most people use, and call the real front of the Bowen the back, and vice versa.)

The Bowen Building was used to house insane women from 1902 to 1908. In 1908, the cottage that would become their permanent home was finished, and they were all moved from the Bowen to their own cottage. The Bowen then became the nurses' building, with big dayrooms and small dorm rooms for the nurses. There were classrooms in the Bowen too, where the finest nursing education program in the country trained the staff of the Peoria State Hospital. In the 1960s, the Bowen was remodeled as an administration building. The big dayrooms and classrooms were partitioned into small cubicles. This incarnation of the building is what you can now glimpse – barely – through the broken windows.

Today, there is a wide stretch of open lawn at the front of the Bowen, with a burn pile in the middle. (The front lawn is used for campouts in the summer, hosted by the Save The Bowen group. After dusk, a crackling bonfire makes a cozy place to roast marshmallows and swap ghost stories.) The lawn slopes off, dropping down to the Mohammed Shriners building and parking lot. This area used to be a sunken garden, and it is the reason that most people, when they remember the asylum, think of the Bowen first.

There were sixty-three garden areas altogether on the hilltop. When visitors to the Peoria State Hospital came to see their relatives, they were invited to sit in the sunken garden. An attendant was sent to fetch the patient, and patient and visitors would chat outside in the lush, peaceful garden, with the elegant stone bulk of the Bowen standing guard behind them. The only part of the hospital to admit visitors was the geriatric ward. Since those patients had limited mobility, it made sense to bring their visitors to them, instead of the other way around. But as a rule, if you had a relative in the asylum, and they weren't elderly, you had your visits in the garden at the Bowen. In nasty weather, or in the wintertime, visits took place at the building which now houses the Phoenix Club.

The people I spoke with that had gone to visit relatives at the hospital were quite young at the time of their visits. The stories they told all came from the 1950s and 1960s, as the facility closed in 1973. The big stone building made a lasting impression on many young minds. This led to the Bowen Building becoming inextricably intertwined with memories of visiting family members. Many people, in their memories of the hilltop, confuse the Bowen Building (which at that time was the administration building) with the asylum proper. For many area residents with ties to the asylum, the Bowen became the defining symbol of the Peoria State Hospital.

Dr. George Zeller loved the Bowen as well. The Bowen was mostly used as an administration building, but it also served as living quarters for the nurses and resident doctors. Dr. Zeller created and nurtured the nurses' college that helped to make the Peoria State Hospital famous in mental health circles. The Bowen was the number-one ranked nurses' college for sixty years, producing the finest nurses in the country. Nurses from the Order of Saint Francis also lived in the Bowen from the late 1960s to its closing in 1973.

Dr. Zeller lived in the Bowen Building with his wife Sophie. Zeller spent many hours in the attic of the building, gazing out across the magnificent view of the bluff, and beyond it, the Illinois River. Dr. Zeller and Sophie occupied an apartment on the third floor of the building, living there until Dr. Zeller's death from pneumonia in 1938. (Sophie had died a few months earlier.) During his final illness, curious people asked Dr. Zeller why he didn't leave the asylum and travel into Peoria for treatment. Dr. Zeller's response was immediate and sensible.

"I'm surrounded by my family, and by the best nurses, and by the prettiest women in the world. Why would I want to leave?"

*"I always felt comfortable ... but I never felt alone."*

Richard Weiss is the current owner of the Bowen. A short, genial man with a neatly trimmed white beard, Richard looks like your favorite uncle. He doesn't look like the owner of one of the most haunted buildings in the country. But he's among the many people that have fallen in love with the Peoria State Hospital, and with this building in particular.

"I saw it listed for sale on eBay, of all places," he says with a shrug. (He didn't actually buy the Bowen on eBay; he went through more conventional channels.)

Richard now heads the Save The Bowen Foundation. He realized very early on that out of the thirteen remaining structures of the Peoria State Hospital, the Bowen was the one most at risk. Old photographs show a stately stone edifice with wide, gracious porches running the length of the building. Today's reality is sadly different. The Bowen has good bones, that much is true. The blocks of limestone have held up well over the years. But the rest of the building is in sad disrepair. There is not one window that still has its glass. The windows stare blankly out over the yard, the lower ones shuttered by sheets of plywood. Pigeons flutter to their nests in the attic through great gaping holes in the roof. The stone walls are sturdy, but the floors and walls inside have been exposed to the elements for decades. Some of the damage is due to the ravages of time and harsh Illinois winters. But the graffiti scrawled on the inside walls is the work of disrespectful human hands. Inside the building, where nurses once eagerly answered questions in class, silence now reigns supreme. It's so quiet you can hear chips of plaster falling off the walls to hit and crumble on the floor.

With the help of many dedicated volunteers, Richard threw himself into raising money for the restoration of the Bowen. The Save The Bowen Foundation opened the building in October 2008, offering ghost tours at $30 for a two hour tour, or $100 for an overnight stay. These tours were led by local paranormal investigators, many of whom had their own experiences inside the building.

Anne Pritchard is the lead investigator for Mid America Ghost Hunters (MAGH). She was the driving force behind getting the TAPS Paranormal team to visit the Bowen in December 2008. The team got to Bartonville after dark on December 19th and launched right into the investigation. They even came back the following day. Kristyn Gartland and two other investigators explored the attic during the day, and heard indistinct whispering. John Zaffis reported feeling uneasy in the basement, which is by far the most active part of the building.

Anne, too, will admit to feeling creeped out down there. "I'll go anywhere else in the building – but not the basement." There's a door in the basement, she told me, that will shut by itself. She was in the basement with a group of investigators when they all saw, at the end of the hall, a shapeless mass of fluorescent aqua-blue mist. The mist formed itself into a glob about four feet high. It came towards the group, then suddenly disappeared. "I've never seen anything like that," Anne said, "and I've never seen it since."

Chris Morris, another volunteer, has also seen a blue mist in the basement. The mist she experienced oozed out of the tunnel at the end of the basement hallway closest to the morgue, hung motionless in the hallway for a moment, then slowly retreated back into the tunnel.

Anne and her group captured recorded evidence in the basement as well. The group was doing some EVP recording in one of the rooms in the basement, and they decided to encourage the spirits by singing. This can be surprisingly effective – maybe music can reach beyond the veil when mere words aren't enough. Anne was crooning the old Tony Orlando and Dawn hit "Knock Three Times". The group's recorders picked up a woman's laugh. They also recorded an indistinct voice trying to sing along to the '70s song – "it sounded like an old drunk guy," is how Anne put it. Eerily, underneath the singing voices, a woman's voice faintly pleaded, "Help me".

Anne has had experiences in other parts of the building as well. The rooms in the Bowen are nearly devoid of furniture. The floors are more usually covered in drifts of broken plaster. But in one room on the first floor, there is still a set of rusty bedsprings, most likely the remains of a mattress dragged there by some nameless homeless squatter sometime in the late 1980s. However the bedsprings got there, they mean something to whatever inhabits that room. Anne's investigators heard the heavy settling *"sproink"* of someone sitting down on the bed, then a creak as they got back up.

One bright fall day, Anne was at the Bowen with another volunteer, Dennis. Dennis was outside mowing the lawn, and Anne was inside the building. She heard the mower stop, so she came out to see if Dennis needed anything. As it turned out, he was just finished with his mowing. He turned towards the building, pulled his camera from his pocket, and snapped a few pictures just for the hell of it. Anne, standing on the porch, waved to him as he clicked away.

Neither of them realized that they were being watched. One of the photos later revealed a face peering out at them from a second floor window.

When the Bowen was open, Anne told me, she would go in by herself all the time. "I always felt comfortable … but I never felt alone."

*"Okay, I feel you …"*

Trish Weiss, Richard's daughter, is a thin, energetic woman whose blonde ponytail bobs as she talks. Trish is always to be found running the Creepy Campouts that the Save The Bowen Foundation hosts several times every summer. The campouts are a fun way for the group to raise money. Admission is $12 per tent. People are invited to pitch their tent and stay all night on the grounds of the Bowen Building. The Save The Bowen group offers soda, water, and snacks for sale. The snacks are fun, portable campout food, like the "Walking Tacos" (ground beef, salsa, shredded cheese, lettuce, tomatoes and onions piled into a bag of corn chips). For the fall campouts, when the bonfire is lit, the group sells "s'mores kits", ziptop bags containing a marshmallow, two graham crackers, and a square of chocolate. A deejay spins tunes until midnight, and the yard of the Bowen echoes with happy activity once again. Campers are encouraged to walk around the Bowen Building and explore the circle path in the woods to the north. Cameras flash, and the red lights of recorders glow, as campers stay up until the wee hours of the morning hoping to witness paranormal activity.

Trish flits from the front porch of the Bowen to the back, then trots a tour group down to Old Book's cemetery at the Pollak Hospital a block away. And while Richard cheerfully claims that he had never had any supernatural experiences whatsoever at the Bowen, Trish will just as cheerfully tell you about everything that's happened to her.

"After one of the campouts, about three o'clock in the morning, my brother Andy, Nick, Candi, Tiffany and I were all standing on the porch by the side door in the back." (Nick, Candi, and Tiffany are also volunteers at the Bowen.) "We could see shadow people moving around in the hallway, which was amazing enough. But then we went over to the basement hole."

Dotted at intervals around the lowest level of the building are square holes, where a brick or two has been left out of the wall. These holes once provided space for the support beams of the Bowen's grand porches. Now they lead directly into the basement. A flashlight beam does little to chase back the blackness, and a chill breeze blows from the depths, smelling of cool damp and forgotten memories.

Trish stuck a DVR (digital voice recorder) into the blackness. Holding it, she asked, "Can you talk into this little red light?" There was silence all around, but later, a raspy male voice came through on the recorder.

*"All right."*

Of course, Trish and the others didn't hear that response at the time. Trish remarked, "I'm not feeling anything."

Telling the story later, she grinned. "I can usually sense something – I feel a little 'creepy'. Obviously I was way off on that one." Obviously she was, because moments later on the recording, another male voice warned, *"Don't come back."*

"Well, of course we gotta go back!" Trish told me. The group moved back to the corner door and tried to coax the shadow people back.

Then they returned to the basement hole. Trish put her hand through the hole again, holding the DVR in the blackness.

"If you're there, can you come up and talk to me?" Trish called out into the darkness.

Suddenly, an icy hand grabbed her arm. Heart racing, Trish said, "Okay, I feel you ..." Seconds passed, and the entity held its cold, invisible grip on her arm. Trish tried to keep her voice steady.

"Can you please let go of me now?" She was starting to get seriously creeped out, caught in the cold grip of who-knew-what down in the basement. Finally her nerve broke, and she yelled, "Let *GO!*"

The entity released its grip on her arm, and Trish pulled her hand out of the blackness. To no one, she announced, "Okay, I am *done* sticking my hand in holes!"

Even after this unnerving experience, Trish has never lost her love for the Bowen and its ghosts. "I'd never caught anything before, no photos, no EVPs. I'd seen plenty, but I'd never captured any evidence – and now we have four EVPs on one tape! Oh, it was so much *fun!*" she gushed, enthusiasm brightening her voice. "Four voices. What more can you ask for?"

*"That's an EVP that I would have put all over the world ..."*

That evening's evidence seemed to be the signal for more entities at the Bowen to reveal themselves to investigators. Trish told me about an EVP her team captured a few weeks later.

"We were up in the attic, and we asked, 'Is there anybody up here with us? Can you tell us your name?' We caught a sweet little girl's voice saying '*Sa-rah!*'" Trish's voice lilted up on the second syllable, and the smile on her face lent brightness to the little girl's name.

"We call her 'Sassy Sarah'. She likes to play with toys, and sometimes she'll tug on people, as if to get their attention. We've gotten her saying '*Mommy*', and '*Can you help me?*'."

Sarah is one of the more vocal ghosts at the Bowen. I spoke with Kristy Carmody at one of the Creepy Campouts in October of 2011.

"See that window over there?" Kristy pointed to the hole leading to the basement. "That first one there, from the left corner of the building. If you leave your recorder running right there, I can almost one hundred percent guarantee you're gonna get something."

Kristy captured an EVP at that basement opening several months before I spoke with her. "What you do is, you put your recorder down and you tell the bad man to let the little girl go." She spoke with the conviction of someone for whom magical thinking is a real, proven concept. "I put a Cheeto down next to the recorder and said, 'Here's a Cheeto for you. Let her go.' I walked away and just left the recorder running as I walked around the grounds for a while.

"I listened to the recording later, to see if I'd gotten anything. I didn't hear a thing for twenty minutes. Then I heard, '*Can you help me?*' It was high pitched, a little girl's voice for sure."

There was frank wonder in her voice. "That's an EVP that I would have put all over the world, if I could. I'd say, 'You have to listen to this,' because it was that clear. You can hear it's not an older person, it's a child."

No one knows why Sarah chooses to hang out in the basement so much, but it's an accepted fact that she does so. People have even tossed playthings down there for her. Sharon Wood filled me in on the details about "Sarah's doll".

"A week before Halloween [2011], someone tossed a doll down into the basement for Sarah to play with. They threw it down the hole nearest the back porch, at the back corner of the building. On Halloween, at the Creepy Campout, we peeked in the hole with a flashlight. The doll was on the opposite side of that basement room, diagonally across from that window." This would have put the doll closer to the hole that Kristy pointed out to me. "The doll was sitting up against the wall, like someone had put here there carefully, not like she'd landed when she was tossed down there. We looked down there on Friday night, and one hand was up to her head. On Saturday night, both hands were up. It was weird." When the Bowen opened back up to the public in October 2012, the *Peoria Journal Star* ran a picture of Richard, Trish, and Sarah's doll on the front page of the paper. The doll's red dress is a splash of color in the dusty basement, and her brown curls seem cheerfully out of place in the gloom.

Kristy Carmody had another paranormal experience at the Bowen earlier that year. She was standing at the top of the stairs leading into the building, and her sister was filming her. As she captured Kristy in the frame, a stream of orbs seemed to flow towards Kristy's midsection. Kristy had recently undergone surgery for ovarian cysts. Were the orbs evidence of a nurse's awareness of her issues? Was a spirit showing concern for her?

Another time, Kristy was walking around the outside of the building taking pictures of the windows, hoping to catch a ghost in one of the shots. With her usual brashness, she yelled towards the building, "Show yourself! I want to see you!" Then she raised her camera and snapped a picture. She looked at the viewscreen – and found herself looking at a figure in the window.

"The camera fell," she admitted. "I was so astounded, I just dropped it."

Kristy's young son has seen one of the Bowen's spirits as well. As Kristy was telling me her tales, her son shared his experience with me as well.

"We drove up to the front of the building. When I was getting halfway out of the car, I saw some man looking out of the window, and he waved at me. But by the time I got out of the car, he was gone." The boy paused, and added in a thoughtful tone, "It was a white guy." (Kristy's son is black.)

The windows of the Bowen are a favorite spot for picture-taking, because spirits often turn up in the photos. One of the most delightful ghost photographs I have ever seen was taken at that very same campout, in June 2011. As I was chatting with people, collecting stories and experiences for this book, someone came up to me and showed me a picture Chris Gibler had just taken with his phone. As soon as I looked at it, and my brain puzzled out what I was seeing, I burst out laughing.

The picture shows a smallish person, maybe a child, but all you can really see at first is the figure's shoulders and the top of its head. Then you realize that what you're seeing is the figure of someone leaning way out over the windowsill of an open window, as if to look down curiously at all the funny people in the yard below. It's a charming picture, and I'm very grateful to Chris for sharing it with me for the book.

Bree Otey, one of the teenage volunteers at the Bowen, has had experiences both with the upper windows of the building and at the basement holes. At one of the campouts, she and several friends were recording very late at night, at the back of the building. Bree said that as they were walking around, they saw "an adorable little girl" in one of the windows. She called out, "Hey guys, stop a second." The group straggled to a halt, and they all looked up at the window.

At the back of the Bowen Building, about in the middle of the building on the second floor, there is a light that comes on at dusk and stays on all night. Through faulty wiring or sheer perversity, the light doesn't stay on all the time – it flickers and stutters, goes off for a while, then blazes back on for several minutes. It was by the light of this cantankerous bulb that Bree saw the little girl.

"She had long blonde hair," Bree told me. "We took a few steps, and so did she. When we stopped, she stopped. It was like she was mimicking us."

(It's not unusual for child ghosts to be hanging out at the Bowen. Dr. Zeller and his staff loved children, and children were allowed to stay with their mothers until the age of four. The Bowen was used to house insane women from 1902 to 1908. Perhaps some of their children came back to the place where they were welcomed in life.)

Earlier that evening, the group had a strange experience at one of the holes leading to the basement. They were using Bree's iPod to do some recording. When they listened to the recording later, they heard a man's deep voice saying, *"I want to touch it."*

The volunteers at the Bowen, even the teens, have taught themselves good ghost hunting practices. Just before that EVP appeared on the recording, Bree had been reminding her friends that touching the iPod while recording could result in unwanted noise on the device. She said aloud, "I'm picking up the iPod and moving it to the other side of the window," just the way a ghost hunter should always do during an investigation.

Five seconds later, a low, deep voice showed up on the recording. *"I want to touch it."*

"It gives me goosebumps just talking about it," Bree told me, "because I know it happened to me."

## The White Lady

At one of the campouts, I was taking a walk around the end of the Bowen Building closest to Pfeiffer Road, when Amanda and her boyfriend called me over. They were standing across the street, staring up at the building's windows. The glassless holes gazed back at us with a blank stare.

Amanda pointed at one of the second floor windows. "She was right there," she muttered.

I shaded my eyes against the glare of the streetlight and peered at the row of windows.

"Who? Which window?"

"Right there." Amanda pointed. "There was a woman there. I could just see the outline of her, but I could see her *eyes*, too. I couldn't look away … she was leaning out of the window, rocking back and forth. Her hands were on the sill, and her hair fell over her shoulders as she leaned forward. Her hair was long, and dark, and kind of stringy, like that girl in *'The Ring'*. And her *eyes* …"

I gazed at her thoughtfully. "You just saw the White Lady," I realized.

It was Trish who first told me of her meetings with the White Lady. Trish has seen her several times, and each time, the experience has been terrifying for her, for reasons she can't really explain.

"She wears a long white nightgown, which is why we call her the White Lady. Her hair is dark and stringy, and it's long. Sometimes I'll see her leaning out of a window, and I can see her hands on the windowsill. Her hair always spills over the sill.

"The last time I saw her, it was two or three o'clock in the morning at one of the campouts. I was on the side porch looking down the hallway. It was dark – the only light was from the bulb over the doorway – but I could see a figure in a white nightgown down the hallway. I felt like she was staring at me, and she tilted her head from side to side as she watched me. Something about the way she did that just seemed menacing – it was *very* creepy.

"I said, 'Come closer,' and she took about five steps towards me. I backed up in a hurry – I didn't want her to get *too* close to me."

Trish laughed as she related this, a short breathy burst of nervous sound. "I'll go and find her for people, but when she's there. I'll always turn my head and look away. She creeps me out. I don't want her noticing me too closely."

Tonya has also seen the White Lady. She went on a tour of the Bowen several years ago with Rob Conover. She was on edge and wired pretty tightly anyway, even though she was visiting during broad daylight. So when she turned to take one last picture of the building, and thought she saw something in one of the windows, she put it down to the tour's spooky influence.

When she got home, though, and downloaded the pictures onto her computer, she knew it wasn't a case of a runaway imagination. There in the window was a woman's face.

"She had long dark stringy hair, with a seventies part," Tonya said. "To tell the truth? She looked psycho. I just got this hateful feeling as she looked at me, like she was staring right through me. It made me stomach drop to somewhere around my knees."

Later, Tonya told Trish about the strange woman. She got an unpleasant shock when Trish took over Tonya's tale, and finished describing the woman Tonya had seen, right down to her long dark hair and her menacing attitude.

Trish's theory is that the White Lady is the ghost of a schizophrenic patient. This theory may have some merit. When the Bowen was first built, it was used to house criminally insane women. One hundred and twenty eight women called the Bowen Building home from 1902 until 1908, when the cottage that would house them permanently was finished. Of course, in those days, a woman could be committed for a myriad of reasons. When we say "criminally insane", we imagine a violent patient, but this wasn't necessarily so. A woman could be committed while suffering from postpartum depression. She could have been in an abusive relationship, and fought back against her abuser, with catastrophic results. At the time these women were living in the Bowen, an insanity decision was handed down by a judge, not a physician. Many of these women came to the Peoria State Hospital from a courtroom. Their case went to trial, they were judged criminally insane, and they were remanded to the asylum instead of being sent to prison.

Could one of these misunderstood women have returned to the Bowen Building, a place where she had found acceptance in life?

Historical facts, though, may point to a different explanation for the appearance of a phantom woman dressed in a long white gown. On October 4, 1915, a housekeeper named Anne M. Stuart fell ill while she was working at the Bowen. She was taken to her room, where she slipped into a coma. She died a few days later of unknown causes. Anne Stuart's death, and the passing in 1938 of Dr. Zeller, are the only two deaths that can be documented as having occurred in the Bowen. And to be fair, Stuart's death may not even count. The newspaper account says simply that she was "taken to her room in the residence hall". The Rose Bigler Hall had opened that year as well. It may be that Anne Stuart died at Rose Bigler, not at the Bowen.

There are other volunteers that have seen the White Lady. They see her not as a threatening spectre, but as a protective spirit. They call her the Singing Lady, and they speak of her not with fear, but with affection.

If you sit quietly in the center of the attic, settle yourself in the silence, and listen carefully, you may hear purposeful shuffling sounds. It will sound as if an invisible someone is bustling around you in the attic, straightening things, putting them away, and generally tidying up. If you are very lucky, you may hear the sound of a woman's voice, softly singing. The song she sings is always "Ave Maria".

Anne Stuart was a housekeeper at the Bowen. Did her duties take her into the attic at times? Some of the nurses' classes had such high enrollment at the beginning of the semester that some of the students had to sleep on cots in the attic. The overflow wouldn't last long, as girls would drop out when they learned how rigorous the training program was. Was Anne one of the housekeepers responsible for tidying the girls' room and changing the bed linens? Many people have heard this unknown entity quietly singing "Ave Maria" as she goes about her duties. Was that one of Anne's habits, singing to pass the time as she worked?

It's a peaceful image – a woman in the white dress and starched apron of a housekeeper, singing quietly to herself as she goes about her business. Quite a different picture from the crazed madwoman that others have described. Whoever the White Lady is, whether she's a benevolent housekeeper or an unbalanced schizophrenic, she is a powerful presence at the Bowen Building. She has been seen many times, and her appearance can be unnerving.

*"Didn't I tell you to leave earlier?"*

The spirits at the Bowen are active at all times of the day and night. The Creepy Campouts, predictably, seem to rile them up. Sharon Wood, who told me about Sarah's doll in the basement, also shared an experience that her daughter had at one of the campouts.

Sharon's daughter and her friend, both in their teens, were standing at the side of the Bowen late in the evening at one of the campouts. They were just chatting, listening to the music the deejay was playing. Suddenly something cold and dark seemed to pass right through them. The friend shuddered; her knees buckled and she nearly fell. Sharon's daughter flinched as the cup of hot chocolate she held was knocked from her hand by the force of the spirit's passage.

Both girls decided to call it a night soon afterwards. They crawled into the tent, shaken, and didn't come out until the next morning.


Paul Gordon, a reporter for *The Peorian* magazine, went on a tour of the Bowen with Rob Conover. This was before the building was closed for asbestos removal. Paul experienced cold spots at random points in the middle of the hallway – "where you don't expect it", is how he put it. He also saw a green glow at the top of a stairwell, something that couldn't be explained by any light source inside or outside the building. The green glow disappeared when people in the group shone their flashlights on it.


Gary and Karen visited the Bowen Building in October 2011. I happened to be there chatting with Richard Weiss that afternoon, and I got to meet the couple.

Gary was standing with his wife at the back of the Bowen, gazing up at the ruined building. He told me that his grandmother had worked here as a nurse, and had gotten his mother a job.

"We moved here from Indiana when I was very young. We didn't have any place to stay, so we lived here in the Bowen Building for a while,"

We chatted for a little while about life at the asylum. Just when I had about given up on getting any ghost stories, Gary surprised me.

"I was here a while ago for a visit, after the asylum closed. We took a picture of a friend of mine standing on the porch, on the other side of the building. The picture showed my friend, and also a small hooded figure next to her. Someone asked me, 'Well, was it your friend's daughter, maybe standing next to her?' I said, 'Not unless you can see through her daughter's head.' The hooded figure was transparent. You could see the bricks of the building right through it. And it had a face like a skull. Honestly? It looked like the Grim Reaper standing next to her."

Debra Collins was walking home from Limestone High School one late spring evening in the 1970s. She happened to look up as she was passing the Bowen, and she saw a light on in the abandoned building. The light stayed on for a few minutes, then went out. It wasn't until the light went out that she saw the outline of a figure standing in the window.

An art student, Cassandra, shared an experience her sister Lindsay had at the Bowen Building. She and Lindsay had gone to Stone Country with some friends for an evening of music and country dancing. Lindsay got bored after a while, and told Cassandra she was going with her friends to walk around the outside of the Bowen, maybe peek in the windows if they could. Cassandra nodded absently, her mind still on the dancing. About five minutes later, she felt someone tugging on her sleeve. It was Lindsay.

"We gotta go," Lindsay muttered, shooting furtive looks around her at the bar patrons.

Cassandra wasn't yet ready to leave, but she humored her sister and they left the bar. On the way home, Lindsay told Cassandra what had happened.

"My friends and I were walking around outside the Bowen, and I looked up. There was some guy leaning out of the window, looking down at me. I freaked out – I had to get out of there."

Chris Morris once saw a full-body apparition in the basement of the Bowen. It was years ago, when she was still exploring the building on the sly. As she passed one of the rooms, she saw a man through the open doorway. He seemed to be engrossed in stacking something on the shelving unit that still stood in the room. Chris nipped past the doorway, trying to avoid being seen. When her friends came up through the tunnels and joined her, she felt courageous enough to go into the room and see who was in there.

She found the room empty.

Years later, when Chris became a volunteer at the Bowen, she was chatting with several nurses who used to work in the building. The nurses all said they'd heard rumors of the ghost of a man who would appear in one of the basement rooms to stack things on the shelves.

Chris and her friends have also had the odd experience of being "shushed" at the Bowen. They were horsing around and being noisy one night, just having a good time, when from nowhere came a stern "SHHH!" The friends all stopped and looked at each other, perplexed.

"You could tell from the look on everyone's face, none of us had made that noise."

Mark Lasswell says he's not psychic, but he is empathic – he can sense feelings. He says that driving down the road between the Bowen and the dining hall, before the hall was torn down, was especially hair-raising – literally.

"I could feel every hair on my body trying to stand on end. Sometimes I'd drive by on purpose, just to feel that electric jolt of fear. It felt bad and kinda good at the same time, you know?"

Harry is one of the volunteers at the Bowen Building. He's known for his fearless approach to ghost hunting. According to his nephew, A.J. Rodgers, Harry has had his nose broken six times by something nasty in the attic of the Bowen. He's also been chased out of the building more than once.

Once, A.J. says, Harry jokingly said to an entity, "Why don't you hop on my back? I'll give you a piggyback ride." Later, Harry suffered from back pain so severe it drove him to the hospital – where x-rays showed that he had two slipped discs.

Stella Link used to help out as a tour guide at the Bowen. One night, the group she was leading was sitting in the morgue, trying to contact the spirits down in the basement. Stella had the creepy sensation of hands touching her legs all over.

Another time, Stella was standing outside the Bowen when she was overcome by feelings of overwhelming sadness. She began to weep without really knowing why.

During one of the tours inside the Bowen in the fall of 2008, a guy on the tour wandered into one of the small rooms on the third floor. He felt an intense sensation of cold all down his right side. He yelled to a friend, "Quick, take a picture of me!"

The picture showed a black shadowy mass engulfing the man's right side. Swirls in the shadows formed the shape of a demonic face.

Karen Tesmond shared a story with me, something that happened to her while she was in the Bowen taking one of the ghost tours. She had wandered away from her group while they were all in the basement. She had gone farther down the hallway, and was in one of the smaller rooms off to the side, when she felt someone tap her shoulder with a gentle insistence.

Her back was to the wall at the time.

Gary Lisman is the author of *Bittersweet Memories: A History of the Peoria State Hospital.* He was in the Bowen with his daughter, and snapped a picture of her with his digital camera. The screen showed some sort of dark mass holding onto her leg.

Melissa, a waitress at a local Hooters restaurant, heard about the strangeness at the Bowen and wanted to see it for herself. She went with some friends to explore the place. They set up a video camera just inside the front door, then walked around the outside of the building for a while.

The camera recorded for about a minute. The sound was working – on the tape, you can hear the group walking away from the camera. Then the picture went fuzzy, and a black shape went across the screen. The camera turned itself off at that point. Melissa says, "It was like something was telling us, 'Ha-ha, we're not going to show you anything!'"

That's all the evidence that was ever found on that recording – even though the camera was running when Melissa and her friends came back to collect it.

A group of ghost hunters was doing an investigation in the Bowen. Two of the investigators, Tara and Jenny, set up a camera in the hallway of the basement, pointing towards the tunnel entrance. Then they left to explore the rest of the building.

The film later showed a mist coming out of the tunnel. It hovered in front of the camera for a moment, then retreated back towards the tunnel entrance. Then the entire screen shook as something unseen bumped the camera.

Ryan M. used to ride his bike with his younger brother and their late uncle when the uncle would come to visit their grandparents in Bartonville every Sunday. One late afternoon, when Ryan was seven or eight years old, the three of them rode their bikes past the Bowen Building. Ryan's younger brother pointed to the building and said,

"Hey look, Ryan, there's a girl in the window up there." Ryan looked up at where his brother was pointing.

A girl in a bright yellow shirt stood in the window, staring down at the three.

"At that point, I figured it was a teenager, since the building wasn't yet boarded up and off-limits. And back then, bright colors were high in fashion, so in my mind, I just passed it off as a teenage girl in a bright yellow shirt."

Recently, Ryan told me, he'd been doing some reading about ghost stories at the old state hospital, when he came across a phrase that triggered that memory from years ago. The story read, "People driving down Pfeiffer Road may see the ghostly figure of a woman with a beehive hairdo in a yellow dress staring down at them."

Stunned, Ryan asked his brother if he remembered pointing at the woman in the window. His brother did remember, and added that the woman had a beehive hairdo.

"Hearing that sent a chill down my spine almost instantly," Ryan told me.

Ryan also shared some of the stranger stories he's heard about the Bowen Building over the years. These stories have more than a whiff of the tall tale about them, but they show what kind of stories can get passed along about a haunted insane asylum over the years.

"I've heard of a table that has ghostly syringes that appear out of nowhere and dispense fluid every hour, and then the plunger goes back up and fills itself up with fluid again before dispensing again an hour later. One guy told me that he heard a story about a ghostly nurse who goes up and down the stairs at night saying 'Where's my patient?' over and over again.

"Another story is of a room that is unusually white, with a lone piano sitting in it. A ghostly lady dressed in white sits at the piano and plays for a while. If the lady turns around and sees someone watching her, she'll ask if they want to learn to play the piano. The person is supposed to say no, but if they do say no, the lady will continue to ask, and will follow the person around asking them over and over again until they finally leave the building. I wasn't told what happens if you do accept the lady's piano lesson, but I imagine it's not a good idea!"

Sam Carter was driving with some friends past the Bowen Building, when the driver stopped the car and dared Sam and a friend to go inside. "We had to go all the way in so we couldn't be seen anymore, in order to prove we had fully entered the building," Sam told me. "We had one flashlight, and I turned it on as we were walking up to the building. It worked fine until we got within maybe fifteen feet of the building – then it began to dim. We stopped and got a little scared since we couldn't see as well. I took a few steps back, and the flashlight got brighter again. So then we started back towards the building and the light dimmed again.

"We decided just to keep going. As we entered the building, the light went out completely. We could barely see, but we made it into the building, hid inside for a few moments, then walked back out. As we were walking away, the flashlight slowly began glowing brighter and brighter. It was a strange experience."

Lisa Gegner, a member of Mid America Ghost Hunters, was a volunteer at the Bowen late in 2008, and helped lead the tours at the building. One evening, she was down in the darkened basement before a tour, and heard a loud male voice moan right in her ear.

Later that same night – Lisa guessed it to be around two o'clock in the morning – she was chatting with another volunteer up on the first floor of the building, in the staging area. It was viciously cold, so Lisa was wearing a pair of Carhartt coveralls. Suddenly, Lisa was tugged backwards by the seat of her heavy pants.

"It was a definite bid for attention," Lisa laughed as she told me the story.

Wesley Theobald is a paranormal investigator in East Peoria. Long before Richard Weiss purchased the Bowen and opened it up for tours, Wesley was one of those kids who went out there in search of excitement. When he was a teenager, he went to the Bowen with five other friends. They broke into the building, armed with a video camera, looking for adventure.

The Bowen did not disappoint them

The group split up, half the guys going up to the third floor. Wesley's group stayed on the second floor. They were filming down the long hallway at the center of the building on the second floor, when one of them yelled, "Did you see that?" A figure made of black smoke, easily seven feet high, had swooped across the hallway, disappearing into one of the rooms.

Suddenly, from the third floor, they heard one of the guys in the other group "scream like a little sissy". "Dude, dude, dude!" was all the guy could say as the friends clattered down the stairs, one of them clutching the video camera. The group gathered around the viewscreen as the cameraman pressed "REWIND" with a shaking finger. The picture jittered backwards for a few moments, then he pressed "PLAY".

The camera focused on the floor, which was covered in a thick layer of white dust, mostly from the plaster that has deteriorated over the years. As the friends watched the footage, bare footprints appeared in the dust, and tracked their way from the middle of the hallway over towards the door to one of the rooms.

The group stuck together after that. They stayed on the second floor, and made their way to the far end of the hallway, camera rolling the whole time. Wesley was doing the filming at that point. He hesitated before telling the next part of the story, as if was almost too personal, too special, too unbelievable to share.

"What I saw next made me fall down," he said simply. The group was in front of a nurses' station at the end of a hallway. Wesley pointed the camera at the glass window of the nurses' station – and filmed a nurse's face looking out of the window at him.

Astonished, he yelled, and the face disappeared. One of his buddies broke into the room to look around. He came out looking pale and shaken.

There was a desk in the office, directly below the window where they'd just seen the nurse's face. The desk was covered with a thick layer of dust, undisturbed for years ... except for a fresh set of handprints. They were small, the handprints of a woman, and they were exactly where someone would have placed their hands to lean on the desk to peer out of the window.

"I keep the footage from that night in a fireproof safe. All my friends have keys, but we don't ever watch it," Wesley told me.

"Seeing it in person was enough."

Stacey Lane was one of the kids who went out exploring, even though it was forbidden. One night, she and her friends were messing around in the steam tunnels that run under the streets of Bartonville, connecting the Bowen with other buildings. Every person in the group had a flashlight. Weirdly, every flashlight died at exactly the same moment.

"I froze where I was. I eventually got my flashlight to work again. I didn't know it, but when the lights went out, everyone else booked out of there, so I was alone. When my flashlight came back on, I heard a noise farther up the tunnel. I looked, and there was a wheelchair rolling towards me.

"I kind of laughed, and yelled, 'If you guys want to scare me, you're going to have to do better than that!' I thought one of my friends had pushed the wheelchair towards me. I found my way out of the tunnel – and everyone was out there waiting for me. I'd been alone down in the tunnel. Well, alone except for whatever pushed the wheelchair."

Ken Hackney is also one of those who went to Bartonville twenty-odd years ago to explore late at night. "We'd park behind one of the buildings so the cops wouldn't find us," he said. Sometimes the atmosphere of the place would be perfectly normal. "Other times, you'd go up there, and it was real heavy in the air, you know? Real spooky."

On one of their nighttime excursions, Ken and a few buddies were walking down the road between the Bowen and the dining hall, which has since been demolished. There was a thick heaviness to the air that night, Ken recalled, and the smell of ozone stung the nose.

As they walked, Ken saw a small red light out of the corner of his eye. Then he saw another. The red dots appeared in the trees on the opposite side of the street from the Bowen Building. Soon others in the group noticed the glowing red dots. "Think the cops set up some kind of infrared surveillance system?" someone muttered.

"There's so many of them, though," Ken said.

An inexplicable feeling of dread gripped the little group, and they decided to cut the night's exploration short. They hurried back to their cars. They were still seeing the glowing red lights as they drove down the street. It wasn't until later that they realized something weird about the glowing red dots.

They were shining out of the darkness of the woods in pairs.

Much more recently, there has been other activity in those woods. There is a circular walking trail cut through the woods directly across the street from the Bowen. It's a short trail – take you five minutes to walk it in the daytime, like Nick Bridges and I did one summer afternoon. But after dark, Nick told me, something else may roam the trail with you.

Some of the female volunteers at the Bowen have claimed to see the glowing form of an older woman along that path. She is solidly built, they say, and she wears her glasses low on her nose – the better to lower a stern glare at anyone she meets along the hiking trail. She'll stare at people as if to say, "What are you doing out of the building?" The girls who have had run-ins with this spirit say the encounter leaves them shaken. They say it's not a pleasant experience.

"I sure don't ever want to meet her," Nick told me.

I wrote about my first visit to the Bowen Building at the beginning of this chapter. But my introduction to the Bowen actually came years earlier.

I was still new to the area, and I had no idea that such a haunted place was so close to Pekin, where my boyfriend lived. (He's now my husband.) We were spending the afternoon together driving around, and he was behind the wheel. He turned to me and asked casually if my 1986 Ford Escort had any mechanical issues.

"Well," I hedged, having no idea where he was headed with the conversation, "it's not a new car. She's got her little quirks, but she gets me from Bloomington to Pekin and back."

"Hmm. There's some place I want to show you, but we can't go if there's any chance the car's going to act up."

That got my attention. Of course, since my husband has no interest whatsoever in paranormal investigation, he really wasn't able to tell me much about the place, beyond the fact that it was a popular place to go exploring late at night. He just said something vague about a haunted insane asylum and left it at that. We didn't end up going to the Bowen that afternoon. I don't remember why – I guess I made enough disparaging remarks about my car's various issues that my boyfriend decided not to trust it around the asylum. But now I knew it was there. I had no idea at the time how important the Peoria State Hospital would become to me.

Derek Waldschmidt, one of the lead investigators with Peoria Paranormal, has also experienced the asylum's tendency to mess with people's cars. He took a girlfriend out to one of the cemeteries once. They wandered around for a while, exploring the old graveyard. Maybe Derek told her the tale of Old Book. But when they walked back to the car and got in to leave, the car wouldn't start. The alternator had suddenly failed, just when Derek had parked the car by the cemetery.

I've met many interesting people over the course of writing this book. One summer evening, I went out to the Bowen after work. When I got there, there was a woman standing in the yard, setting up a tripod and aiming a camera at the upper floors. Merilee Mitchell is a photographer and filmmaker from LA, and she had been drawn to visit the Bowen while in Illinois dropping her son off at camp.

Merilee's son was attending some sort of summer camp in Peoria, and she had flown out to drop him off. She'd decided to spend a few days sightseeing in the area, and she experienced a strange pull to come to Bartonville. Driving up Pfeiffer Road, she encountered the looming bulk of the Bowen, and she just knew she had to stop, get out, and take some pictures of the lovely old building.

Merilee is very sensitive, and it wasn't long at all before she realized there was something unusual about the beautiful stone building. She started taking photographs at the back of the building.

"I started taking pictures that morning, and it was beastly hot. There was a man in a white gown that was following me all around the yard as I was trying to shoot," she told me. "I got a sense of extreme paranoia from him, like he really didn't want me there. I came back later that afternoon, when it wasn't quite so hot, and the same guy was there. He said, *'You mean you're back here again? Didn't I tell you to leave earlier?'* He was really upset with me."

Merilee moved from the back yard of the Bowen to the side porch – the same porch from which Trish often sees the White Lady. Merilee tried twice to shoot pictures near that door. Both times she had to turn away. "The energy coming out of there was just too powerful."

She moved across the street, near the trees. She says she was standing there fiddling with her camera and tripod. She looked up at the building to frame her shot and she saw an apparition "just go gliding by".

*"There's too many people here ..."*

Along with spirit photography, one of the biggest draws of the Bowen Building is the wealth of EVPs that have been captured there. The Save the Bowen group held their first fundraiser on September 27, 2008. They invited former employees to come back to the Bowen, and they spent four hours taping interviews with those employees.

According to Richard Weiss, that four hour tape contains around seven hundred distinct EVPs.

There are between thirty-two and thirty-six different spirits that are active at the Bowen, and they are not shy about speaking up for a recorder. Richard was one of several people that were interviewed for a documentary called *For the Incurable Insane*, a project that is the brainchild of Janette Marie. In the film, Richard mentions the wealth of EVPs that can be captured at the Bowen Building. Richard sits at the front door of the Bowen, and says, "If you leave a recorder running in this building, you'll be amazed at what you'll hear," and smiles. Immediately, a whispered *"Yeah"* is heard in response. How perspicacious of the spirits, to chime in during the filming of a documentary!

Some of the EVPs that have been captured at the Bowen Building are just charming. Some investigators, like Anne Pritchard, have used music to draw out the spirits at the Bowen. A woman told me that she and a friend had brought a CD player to the building, and they had sat on the lawn for a while letting a recorder run while they played a CD of ragtime music. They captured the sound of a woman's voice laughing in sheer delight at the sprightly, lilting music.

Kristy Carmody shared a few more delightful EVP stories with me. She and her sister were wandering around outside the building, recording as they walked. At one point, a woman's voice, tinged with curiosity, asked, *"What are they up to?"* Later on, Kristy suggested that it was about time to turn the recorder off and leave. Her sister said no, let's leave it running for a few more minutes, because you never know what you're going to catch right at the end of a session. Moments before the recording ends, there's a lilting, friendly *"Hel-lo!"* as a female spirit greets them.

One of the very best EVPs that I've ever collected showed up on my recorder when I wasn't expecting it. It was just one of those happy accidents. I was deep into the research for this book, and I went to the Bowen in October 2011, when the Haunted Infirmary had just started up at the Pollak Hospital, a block away. The Save The Bowen group had decided to put on a massive ghost hunt on the first Saturday in October. Over two hundred people showed up, and the organizers decided to split everyone into four groups. The groups would rotate between the Bowen and the three cemeteries, which are all within walking distance. Between the crowd gathered at the Bowen, and the hordes of people waiting in line to go through the Haunted Infirmary, that little piece of Bartonville was one hopping place.

Rather than follow just one group around, I decided to stay at the Bowen and let people come to me with their stories and experiences. I had my notebook out and my recorder going, so I looked like I was there to do some sort of research.

I was chatting with Trish Weiss and Kristy Carmody at the back of the building, where the wonky light is. Trish had told me about getting her arm grabbed, and Kristy had shared with me the story of hearing the little girl in the basement say "I need help!" It was nearly midnight, and Kristy still had an hour's drive home to Bloomington.

It was just the three of us saying our goodbyes, since Kristy's husband and young sons had already gotten into the car. So the recorder should have just picked up three female voices, saying things like, "Glad you could come out tonight," "It was great seeing you again," "Have a safe trip home," ordinary conversation like that.

Which it did – but underneath our three female voices is a hoarse, male whisper.

*"There's too many people here, there's too many people here."*

I reviewed the recording later, in order to jot down notes for the book. So many people had shared so many stories with me; I was congratulating myself on having the foresight to have the recorder going as I chatted with everyone who had come up to me with an experience to share. When I heard that low, urgent whisper, I sat up straight in my chair as my jaw hit the table. I rewound the recording and listened again. There it was. I could just picture a patient standing next to us, wringing his hands in a constant, fretful gesture, complaining out loud to anyone who would listen that "there's too many people here".

*The Basement*

By far the most notoriously active part of the Bowen Building is the basement. The flat smell of old plaster and damp stone is most noticeable down there. The fact that the morgue is down in the basement is enough to give most people the heebie-jeebies right off the bat. (Remember that the Bowen was for many years the finest nurses' college in the country. Autopsies were performed in the morgue on occasion for teaching purposes. The nursing students took part in one, maybe two autopsies a year.)

We've heard about Sarah and her doll. There seem to be other entities that inhabit the basement too, spirits that are not as innocuous as a little girl who likes to play with dolls.

There are stories about a black shadowy mass that chases people out of the basement. Trish Weiss says that she herself has been chased up the stairs by the threatening spectre. And the basement is the one place in the building that Anne Pritchard, an experienced investigator, refuses to go by herself.

I had my own encounter with the unknown in October 2011. It was the night of the massive ghost hunt, the same evening that netted me the crystal-clear *"there's too many people here"* EVP. Much later, at about two o'clock in the morning, I was standing at one of the holes leading down into the basement. People were still milling around excitedly in the dark, even at that late hour. Several teenage girls had wandered over to stand with me, and they were sharing their experiences as we gathered around the hole in the wall.

"Oh, you have a flashlight. I was like –" The girl's casual story was interrupted by a sound from the basement. She looked at me, sharp concern flashing in her eyes.

"You heard that, right?"

"I did, yes," I said. I thought it was ironic that she'd turned to me for confirmation, since I was just about to ask her the same thing. "That came from *inside* the building." Excitement mingled with nerves in my voice, I could hear it.

We all looked warily at the square black hole. My recorder sat on the wide stone ledge of the hole, but I made no move to pick it up. Trying to keep my voice steady, I called down into the basement.

"Can you make that noise for us again?"

Immediately a sudden noise came from down in the basement. It was a sharp metallic clang, like a large bolt being thrown against the stone wall – "*ta-TING!*" All of us jumped back about three feet from the dark hole. Our choreographed Scooby Doo-and-Shaggy impression would have been funny to anyone watching – and it was funny to us, too, once our hearts started back up again.

But whatever was down there wasn't done playing with us. About five minutes later, Nick Bridges, one of the volunteers at the Bowen, came to check on us. We described to him what we'd just heard from the depths of the blackness. "Really?" he said, intrigued.

Just then another two sharp knocks came from the basement hole, as if something down there was letting us know that it was listening.

"It sounds really … *dense* in there," I said.

"Yeah. I keep thinking about Trish putting her hand through that hole and getting grabbed," Nick said.

Someone else shrugged. "If there's something down there, that'd be a perfect way to find out …"

Nobody seemed too keen to follow up on this suggestion.

Unfortunately, there is a very good reason for people to experience feelings of evil and dread in the basement of the Bowen Building. In the 80s and early 90s, the village of Bartonville had a terrible problem with Satanists breaking into the Bowen and holding dark, horrifying rituals inside. These thrill-seekers stirred up entities and powers that they couldn't even hope to understand, much less control.

When the Save The Bowen Foundation purchased the building, they brought in practitioners of three different faiths. A Wiccan, a Jew, and a Christian naturalist all went through the building together, and cleansed it according to their beliefs. They performed a sage smudging to purify the building. Besides being delightfully fragrant, sage is considered a very strong herb in a magickal sense. Practitioners feel that sage can lend its strength to magickal workings. They feel that by burning a bundle of dried sage and letting the smoke permeate a place, the essence of the sage will purify the area. They also sunk a blessed newel post made of solid iron into the floor of the basement. They placed the iron post next to the stair leading up to the front door, to form a spiritual barrier to prevent any malevolent energy from making its way up the basement stairs and out of the building.

*"The Bowen protected the rest of us ..."*

It's not hard to see the appeal of the Bowen. Quite honestly, it has distinct moods. Seeing it in the bluster of a gray November, or the blackness of Halloween night, is much different than seeing it on a sunny day in high summer. It can be chilly and foreboding, sullenly brooding over its secrets. It can be warm and welcoming, its creamy limestone almost glowing in the late afternoon sun.

Even unyielding skeptics notice the changeable moods of this building. A friend of mine who used to come out here with his buddies to go exploring told me this years ago. He said that he and his friends would come out here and park, then sit in the car for a while, trying to gauge what kind of mood the asylum was in that night. Sometimes, he said, after a few minutes you realized things were perfectly fine, and you could get out of the car, go into the building, and explore all night long. At other times, though, the air felt heavy, oppressive. You got the feeling that *something* didn't want company that evening. On nights like that, you didn't wait around to see if the atmosphere changed, and you did not ask questions. You left. Right away.

The Bowen is such a grand old building, even in its current state of decay. Broken windows notwithstanding, the stone blocks give off a sense of permanence, almost like the regal timelessness of a medieval cathedral. The thought that this gorgeous piece of history could be taken away – that it could be torn down – is just devastating to the fans of the Bowen.

Now, though, it looks like the Bowen will live on. The asbestos has been abated, thanks to the funds provided by the town of Bartonville. The Bowen is now open to the public and available for tours. (Information can be found at the Fractured Spirits Facebook page, or at www.peoria-asylum.com.) There are plans to turn it into a bed and breakfast at some point in the future. For now, though, people are content to simply wander through the building looking for ghosts.

"The Bowen protected the rest of us," Chris Morris insists. Because of its solid visibility, and most likely, its proximity to Pfeiffer Road, the Bowen became a magnet for curiosity seekers after the asylum closed. No other building took the abuse that the Bowen suffered. Fueled by stories of ghosts and insanity, troublemakers broke into the beautiful old building. They scrawled graffiti on the walls and vandalized the place. Worse yet, they used the Bowen for dark rituals, inviting things into this world from beyond the veil – things they didn't understand, and could not control.

"The Bowen took the brunt of the abuse. When vandals and Satanists used the asylum for their evil games, it was the Bowen they broke into. They pretty much forgot about the other buildings. That really saved the rest of us from a lot of the damage. She sacrificed herself for the rest of us," Chris says, fondness and respect in her voice.

# THE POLLAK HOSPITAL

*"You get a bunch of teenagers in here, with all that energy, this place comes alive."* -- *John Callear, speaking of the Pollak Hospital*

When Dark Continents Publishing launched the first baker's dozen of books in its product line, the president of the company decided to do some good. I've known David M. Youngquist for several years, and he loves the written word with a clear, undeniable passion. At his suggestion, the company decided to donate one copy of each book in its catalog to two area libraries. One, up in David's neck of the woods, was the tiny Sheffield Library. Dark Continents' donation of thirteen books covered three-quarters of their book purchasing for the year.

The other library chosen to receive a full complement of books was the library I work for, Fondulac District Library in East Peoria. Our director was thrilled with the donation, and called the local paper in to take pictures. David drove down from Princeton with a back seat full of books. Since it was a drive of an hour and a half for him, he asked me to suggest other area libraries for him to visit that morning. The plan was for David to make Fondulac his first stop, donate the books, then visit a few more libraries. Then he'd drive back to East Peoria, meet me for lunch, then drive home.

I gave him detailed directions, sending him from East Peoria to Pekin, then across the river to Alpha Park Library in Bartonville. Now, David's a sensitive. As I handed him the sheet of directions, I said, "Okay, now after you cross the river and go north into Bartonville, you're going to turn left at the first stoplight and go up a hill. At the top of the hill you're going to pass a great big stone building on your right. Put your guards up – I'm not kidding about this."

Halfway through my morning, I got a text message from David.

*Was there a TB ward at this hospital you keep telling me about?*

*Yup. It was called the Pollak Hospital.*

*Thought so. I picked up a hitchhiker.* ☺

Later, over lunch, David told me the whole story. He had been driving up Pfeiffer Road, and was just passing the Bowen, when he felt a heavy tightness in his chest. Then he became aware of someone sitting in the passenger seat of his truck. It was a lanky guy, dressed in workingman's clothes.

"You know how you can tell an old farmer by his hands? Their hands are big, callused, with swollen knuckles from a lifetime of work. I could tell this had been a big guy, but he'd gotten sick later in life."

David said, "Um … hello there. My name's David … what's yours?"

"*George*," came the reply.

"What's the problem, George?"

"*I've got TB.*"

Given the sympathetic tightness in his chest, David had been expecting that answer. "When did you die?"

This question didn't get an answer. The shade in David's passenger seat was silent. David figured that either George didn't know he was dead, or he didn't feel like discussing it. He tried another question.

"You're not coming home with me, are you?"

*"No, this is my home."*

"So ... why are you in my car?"

An ethereal shrug. *"I don't get out much."*

David gave a mental snort. *Wait, what? You're an incorporeal being! Whaddya mean "you don't get out much"?* But David's a nice guy, and he didn't object to George riding along with him. The Alpha Park Library is still technically on the grounds of the old asylum, so George wasn't going off of the grounds without a pass or anything like that.

David did his library visit, although he told me he felt a little funny about it. As he talked with the librarian, he kept casting surreptitious glances over his shoulder, trying to make sure George didn't wander too far away. He didn't want to leave the guy behind. After leaving the library, David and George rode all the way back down Pfeiffer Road together. At the bottom of the hill, George said, *"Well, thanks for putting up with me."* Then he vanished from the passenger seat.

"He was very cordial," David said. "He was one of the most pleasant, well-behaved spirits I've ever encountered."

*Haunted Portajohns*

The Pollak Hospital was built in response to a study conducted at the Peoria State Hospital in 1939. The hospital was named after Dr. Maxim Pollak, who discovered that 95% of the population of the

Peoria State Hospital – both patients and staff – had some form of tuberculosis. Throughout the asylum's seven decades of operation, tuberculosis was the number one killer of patients. (Old age and general decrepitude was the second most common cause of death, and pellagra was the third.) Even with the study, which showed a desperate need for a ward dedicated to the treatment and care of tuberculosis patients, it wasn't until ten years later that the hospital was built. The building went up in 1949, and opened in 1950. Before that, a solarium stood on the site.

The Bowen Building looms over Pfeiffer Road with its creepily imposing stone bulk and the vacant stare of a hundred knocked-out windows. The Pollak, on the other hand, looks like an abandoned grade school. On the surface, the Bowen has a much higher creep factor than the Pollak does. But for my money, the Pollak is much more haunted than the Bowen. For starters, Cemetery 2 is right next door to the Pollak, mere steps away from the front door to the building.

Hell, even the portajohns at the Pollak are haunted. The guides at the building have sworn to me several times that sometimes, when you're in the minty box doing your business, a voice will whisper a rough "*Hey!*" in your ear. (All I can say is that if it ever happens to me, it will be a very good thing that I've already got my pants down around my ankles, if you know what I mean.)

Sam Callear, the son of the present owner of the building, told me on one of my visits that one of the two portajohns had been locked from the inside earlier that evening, although it turned out to have no one in it. Maybe ghosts like a little privacy now and then.

And once, three of the guides, Stacy, Andrew and Trudi, were in the Men's Ward when they heard children laughing and giggling and horsing around. They went outside to check out the noises, but there were no children around the building. They did, however, hear the

139

noisy crunch of leaves under small feet behind the portas – but again, there were no living human beings sneaking around the boxes.


*Looking for Daddy*

The Pollak has been the site of many, many deaths over the years. This is another fact that argues for the Pollak being far more actively haunted than the Bowen, which was an administration building and nurses' apartments. Over four thousand people passed away within its walls. There were three to five deaths a week in the building over the span of twenty-two years. The Pollak's floor plan reflects this awareness of the virulent nature of tuberculosis. The two wards, men at one end of the building and women at the other, are both further divided into two sections. Upon admittance, the tuberculosis cases were segregated into patients that had at least a chance of survival, and hopeless cases. The doctors didn't want to distress any patients that had a fighting chance with the sight of the pallid faces of those at death's door.

Still, the death toll at the Pollak was appalling. Tuberculosis does not only attack the lungs, as in pulmonary tuberculosis (known in earlier times as consumption). It can also involve the brain or spinal cord (meningitis, encephalitis). People with alcoholic liver disease (cirrhosis) are at an increased risk of TB. (The Peoria State Hospital was also one of the premiere clinics for the treatment of alcoholism.) TB can also cause liver failure (hepatitis). Researchers in the early twentieth century discovered, oddly enough, that schizophrenic patients were more prone to catch tuberculosis. It is a nasty, vicious disease.

If tuberculosis struck a household, it was likely to affect more than one member. At times, entire families were admitted to the hospital. The spread of the disease was hastened by hand-me-downs. TB germs are transmitted, among other vectors, on clothing. So if one person contracted tuberculosis and died, and their clothes got passed down to other family members who could use them, those other unfortunates got a good unhealthy dose of TB germs along with Grandma's cardigan or Uncle's overalls.

A tour of the Pollak invariably begins at the end of the hallway near the Men's Ward. Chris Morris stands at the door to the patient intake room, describing the procedure by which patients were admitted to the hospital.

"They came in through this door, into this decontamination room. They were asked to remove their clothing, which was then taken out back and burned. Then they were given a cold-water douche." She says this with a look of bland innocence, waiting several beats for the inevitable squirms from the female members of her audience, before she relents. With a grin, she points out that "douche" is simply an old-fashioned word for "shower".

"Every patient was given a warm bath and then a cold shower. The temperature of the bath was actually prescribed by the doctor." This method of treatment, a hot bath followed by a cold shower, opens the pores of the skin to release toxins, then closes them quickly. It was felt to be invigorating and therapeutic, and it's still a fad in some health circles today.

The Pollak took in all of the TB patients who didn't have the money to go to a hospital in Peoria. It served not only mental patients, but also people from the surrounding communities. The Pollak admitted patients of all ages, from grandparents down to little kids.

There are several child ghosts at the Pollak, including a little girl whose voice was recorded in the Men's Ward. The investigator says, "Is there anyone in here? ... Is there anyone in here? ... Anyone want to say something?" After that third invitation, a girl's voice says "*In here!*" Shortly afterwards, a male voice sternly says, "*Get back.*" Was it a warning to his little girl not to talk to strangers?

I asked Chris, the unofficial historian of the Peoria State Hospital, what a little girl would have been doing in the Men's Ward.

"She's probably looking for Daddy," Chris said. "TB usually killed several family members if it hit a household. Tuberculosis really was the Black Death of its time." Tuberculosis still kills around a million people a year worldwide.

The symptoms of tuberculosis are also responsible for some of the more spectacular paranormal experiences in the Pollak. Several people have reported tasting blood in their mouths. Pulmonary tuberculosis causes lesions in the lungs. Coughing can cause these lesions to rupture, spilling blood into the lungs. A classic symptom of consumption, or TB, is coughing so hard that the patient coughs up blood. Some people are so nauseated by the taste that they have to leave the building and go outside to vomit in the grass. Stacy Carroll, one of the guides at the Pollak, has tasted blood in her mouth as she came up the stairs from the basement of the building.

Danielle, an investigator with Illinois Ghost Seekers Society, was the first person to tell me about the taste of phantom blood. Danielle also shared another paranormal experience with me – and again, it was a sensory anomaly.

"I was sitting in the Men's Ward with several other investigators. We were asking questions, trying to get some EVPs, when we all noticed this weird smell around us. It was a little bit of cinnamon, mostly pine. It smelled like Christmas."

It took me several moments to process this. Once I did, my eyes widened in recognition. The Pollak operated in the mid-twentieth century, and like the rest of the Peoria State Hospital, it used alternative therapies as well as conventional medicine. In herbal medicine, white pine is one of the best decongestants there is. Watkins, the revered natural products company, still uses white pine oil in its cough syrup. I'm absolutely convinced that what Danielle and the other investigators smelled that evening was a whiff of some long-ago chest liniment, or the aroma of a dose of cough medicine.

*"Heavy boots!"*

This all seems to happen in the Men's Ward. The Men's Ward is the more spectrally active of the two wards. There is a spirit in the Men's Ward that clomps around in a pair of heavy boots, like the ugly but serviceable shoes of a workingman. Chris was closing up after a tour of the Pollak one evening. She was in the delousing entryway through which patients were first brought into the building, where they were required to stand for decontamination. The lights in the building had all been turned off, and Chris was relying on a small flashlight that Jeff, her coworker, was holding. The two of them were making sure that the building was secure for the night, when Chris heard the *"clomp clomp clomp"* of booted feet. She was convinced that she had inadvertently locked someone in the building – someone who was not at all happy about finding himself suddenly in the dark in a haunted tuberculosis ward.

Chris hissed to Jeff, "Give me the light." He didn't hear her, and the footsteps were getting closer. "Give me the light," Chris muttered, a little louder. She just knew there was an angry haunted house patron headed her way, stomping his way up the hall, ready to tell her off for locking him in the hospital in the dark.

"GIVE ME THE LIGHT!" Chris bellowed. Startled, Jeff swung the flashlight towards her ... and the furious footsteps came to an abrupt halt. Chris looked up and down the dark hallway, playing the flashlight beam across the tiles, searching the dancing shadows for the big angry man she was sure had just been stomping up to her.

Chris' furious patron was invisible.

Chris has become sensitive to the building's ghostly inhabitants, but this one caught her flat-footed. She usually feels the fine hairs on the back of her neck prickle when a spirit is near, but this time, she had absolutely no warning. Finding that her "big angry guy" was a phantom, she shook her head. "Okay, you got me," she admitted with a sheepish grin.

That's not the only time the ghost with the heavy boots has made his presence known. Stacy was in the Haunted Infirmary attraction one evening after close when she had her own run-in with the spirit.

In the haunted house display, there are deep barrels with lightbulbs in the bases, to give the impression that they glow from the inside. Stacy had reached down into the last barrel and had unscrewed the lightbulb when another haunt worker turned off the lights to the building, plunging the Men's Ward into blackness.

"I thought, okay, do I reach back into the barrel and feel around and screw the lightbulb back in by feel, or do I make my way back down the hallway in the pitch dark?" Stacy said. In a moment, though, someone else made the decision for her. She heard the clomp of menacing footsteps headed her way, and she took off running.

Halfway down the hall, in one of the other rooms, Chris looked up, startled, as Stacy raced past her. Stacy gasped out, "Heavy boots!" and kept booking down the hallway. That was all the explanation Chris needed.

Chris has her own theory as to why Heavy Boots wanders the halls of the Pollak.

"One of the most basic human emotions is fear. Nothing compares to it. Fear will make you do things nothing else will – have you ever heard of someone crapping their pants when they're sad? And if that's what these spirits feed on, human emotions, well, that's the strongest, most basic one there is. We're scared of the monster under the bed long before we ever fall in love. Maybe they get a 'charge' out of that, out of the way your body reacts when you're terrified. They scare people, they bring out that fear ... and that works for them."

*What's in the attic?*

I've had my own experiences with ... well, with whatever haunts the Men's Ward. One evening I joined an informal investigation, just a few of us with cameras and digital recorders. We were all sitting in the Men's Death Ward, in the room that now serves as a garage and as storage for the wood used in building the sets for the Haunt. This was where the most advanced cases of TB were brought, the patients who had only weeks to live, perhaps only days. The atmosphere was quiet and a little tense. One of the investigators, Liz Yost, said that she kept seeing a dark, menacing shadow lurking in one corner of the room. It bothered her so much that she got up from where she was sitting and changed seats, trying to escape the phantom's silent regard. "It's a little less irritating over here," she explained from the far side of the room.

The energy was off-kilter; even I could feel that something wasn't quite right. We could feel *something* watching us, waiting, biding its time ... but whatever it was, it was being very quiet. At one point, I spoke aloud.

"Okay, you guys know I'm writing a book. It doesn't feel like there's much going on tonight. I need stories for the book, fellas." I paused.

"Come on, guys, can you make a noise for us? I need you to really wow me!"

Moments later, we all heard a heavy, *settling* sort of noise from the attic directly above us. It sounded like someone sitting down heavily in a creaky chair, but it encompassed the entire ceiling.

"There was your 'wow' moment," Stacy muttered.

"Guess so."

"That guy keeps staring at me." Liz had moved back to her original seat, but she kept shooting nervous glances towards the darkest corner of the room.

"You know what?" someone said. "This just feels wrong. The energy, you know, it's just … off." Several people agreed. *Ominous* was the word that we all kept returning to. Suddenly, we all agreed that "out of the room" seemed like a very good place to be, and we all left in a hurry. No one was scared, but there was a silent consensus that we all simply wanted to be out of that part of the building.

As I went out of the room, I could have sworn that there were two people behind me. But when I looked closer, Liz stood alone in the doorway, pointing her camera back into the room. The flash went off, and she lowered the camera and yelled irritably, "Don't follow me! Stay there!" Later, she told me that she had hung back on purpose. She could feel the menacing presence right behind her, and she wanted to see if she could capture it on camera. She waited until everyone else had scuttled out of the room ahead of her, because she didn't want to blind anyone with the flash. "I was the last one out of that room," she assured me.

The energy in the Women's Ward is quieter, gentler, but still active. Investigators often hear music in the hallway leading to the Women's

Ward. Stacy and her husband were walking down the hallway when her husband put his hand on her arm and said, "Wait … stop for a second." Moments later they both heard whistling down the hallway.

Stacy herself has heard humming, which then changed to a woman's voice repeatedly singing "Oh, can I let down my hair?"

"I think she made that up. She was just singin' away," Stacy said.

### The Dirty Girl

One of the entities in the Women's Ward is quite a bit livelier than the others. Chris and Stacy jokingly call her "the dirty girl". A medium who was doing a walkthrough of the Women's Ward paused, and said to Chris, "Ooh, you've got a nasty one here. You've got a spirit in here that likes the boys, don't you? I mean *reaaallly* likes the boys?" She made a suggestive cupping motion with her hand. Chris, grinning in spite of herself, nodded.

Several weeks before, during a ghost hunt, one of the Limestone JFL coaches had come up to Chris and muttered, "These ghosts … can they grab your, uh, package?"

Chris shrugged. "They can grab anything they want."

The coach's wife set her lips in a thin line. "Gimme that." She grabbed the K-II meter, which measures electromagnetic energy – ghosts, essentially. She shoved it nearly in her husband's crotch.

The meter pegged up past five and started beeping madly. She moved it away, and the needle dropped. She swung it back to his privates, and the needle rose again.

The Dirty Girl seemed to be enjoying herself.

The entity in the Women's Ward isn't the only "handsy" spirit at the Pollak. Jackie McDowell, one of the volunteers, was at the building for a work party one night. A bunch of high school volunteers were there too, many hands making light work. Jackie and the kids had been painting the haunt, and had been boogying down to happy, danceable '80s music. They took a snack break, and all the kids crowded into the small room off to the left of the entrance hallway. (This is the same room where the guys from Living Dead Paranormal were sleeping when something lifted their cots a foot off the floor, then banged them down again.) The kids were laughing and chatting, and Jackie was leaning against the door jamb, her mind still off dancing to that '80s beat.

"Out of nowhere, I got goosed, and I mean good. I could feel a hand – four individual fingers and a thumb – and whoever it was grabbed a healthy handful of bottom." Jackie jumped, but she laughed off the experience. There are just some really playful spirits at the Pollak.

The ghosts there certainly do like their fun. They especially love scaring the paste out of new visitors to the building. On one of my many visits, I was with Chris, Merilee Mitchell (the photographer from LA), and Sharon Wood, whom we'd met at the Bowen and who had told me the story of the doll in the basement there. The four of us were chatting in the room off of the entrance hall – the room where Jackie got goosed – and while Chris, Merilee and I were perfectly fine, Sharon kept jumping and brushing at her arms and legs, glaring behind her every time.

"Someone keeps grabbing me," she complained.

"Darn it, why is it I hardly ever get touched?" I groused. "I'm right here, guys, you could grab me once in a while, you know."

Chris grinned. "They're used to you. They know *I'm* not gonna jump. And Merilee can see them, so it's no fun for them to sneak up on her. Sharon's the newbie."

Sharon sighed as she swatted irritably at her calf. "Lucky me."

There's a certain kind of touch visitors to the Pollak might experience, Chris explained. The nurses at the Peoria State Hospital were trained in techniques of gentle persuasion. If a patient was found wandering around where they weren't supposed to be, a nurse would place her hand on the patient's shoulder, a friendly gesture that reminded them to behave. If the patient didn't come along quietly, the nurse would then put her hand firmly on the patient's upper arm and guide them to where they were supposed to be.

If an investigator, or even a casual visitor to the Pollak, is walking around a part of the building that a nurse might consider off-limits, they might feel the touch of a friendly hand on their shoulder. And if they ignore that touch, and continue to explore, they might feel a further firm grip on their arm. It's probably a nurse, still going about her duties, politely reminding them with a touch that they should move along now.

*"This place comes alive."*

The Pollak Hospital is now owned by the Limestone Junior Football League. John Callear is nominally the owner, and his son, Sam, is a regular visitor to the building. The JFL puts on a haunted house in the building every October as a fundraiser, and there are plans to use the building for other events as well. Movie nights are a big hit, and there are ghost tours throughout the year. It helps that the cemetery where Old Book is buried is just yards away from the building, down a gentle slope. A Zombie Massacre is planned for October. Participants are given laser tag guns, and are let loose to wreak havoc on a horde of approaching "zombies" – staggering, groaning actors in full horror-movie makeup, volunteers who don't mind taking a shot or two in the name of entertainment.

Construction on the haunted house goes on all year round, as the organizers and actors hone their craft and brainstorm even better ways to scare the paste out of people. The warm friendly smell of freshly cut wood is a faint, constant presence in the hallways of the Pollak. Set builders rip two-by-fours to form a walk-through maze that will disorient haunt-goers every October. The mazes and frights go up one sheet of plywood at a time. The makeup artists have gotten their technique down to a science. During its first year of operation, The Haunted Infirmary placed eleventh in a state-wide haunted house contest, and was also voted "Best New Haunted House" in Illinois. The Haunted Infirmary promises to be a staple of local Halloween flavor for years to come.

The floors, the ceilings, the walls, the paint on the doors, it's all original. With the exception of the haunt sets, the interior of the Pollak remains just as it was left when the building was shuttered in 1973. One of the doors is even painted a gentle shade of lavender, a reminder of Dr. Zeller's use of color therapy to calm unruly patients. The building itself is in an excellent state of preservation, unlike its unlucky sister, the Bowen. Inside, the basic structure is what the patients would have seen in their time there. The JFL uses temporary sets for the Haunted Infirmary. Aside from the haunt, they try to keep the building in as original a state as possible. This is done to aid the paranormal investigators who flock to the building.

The Haunted Infirmary is home to many more spooks than just the ones in greasepaint and latex. "You get a bunch of teenagers in here, with all that energy, this place comes *alive*," John Callear told me. Sam, his son, is one of the teenage volunteers that make the Haunted

Infirmary such a popular place every October. Sam's post one year was in one of the "exam rooms".

"There's a file cabinet in there, and the drawer would keep opening," Sam said. "Our job was to pop out of the room and scare people. I'd go back into the room, and the drawer would be open. I'd close the drawer, we'd huddle in the room until the next group came by. We'd come running out to scare them, and every time we went back into the room, the drawer would be open again." Draven, Chris's son, eventually couldn't handle it and told Sam he was scared to be in that room. "That drawer keeps opening. I don't like it," Draven said.

Down the hallway, closer to the middle of the building, is a room the haunters call The Office. It's paneled in warm knotty pine, and on the walls hang several of those joke Halloween pictures, the holographic portraits that morph from normal photographs into grinning skulls. A couple of jars display gory, gooey-looking "specimens" floating in cloudy liquid. The Office is a spacious, well-lit room that investigative teams like to use as Command Central.

But dark energy lurks in the Office too. Sam politely but flatly refuses to go into that room, even when all the lights are blazing. He told me he once saw a dark, menacing shadow in the corner. Another time, he saw several pieces of chalk go flying off of the chalkboard rail. The experience spooked him so badly that now, he won't go in there.

Over a decade ago, when the building was being used as offices for Nepco, a window and door company, a woman had her office in this room. There was activity in the room even then – spirits would regularly knock things off of the woman's desk.

An unsettling EVP has also been captured in the Office. Several investigators were doing some recording. Speaking of the spirits they were attempting to contact, one of the ghost hunters said, "I think they're sad." A male voice then retorted, *"I'm angry."*

This energy just increases in October, when the haunt is in full swing. A group of three women was chatting on their way out of the building, when they heard a man's voice say, *"We're right behind you."*

Another woman came out of her trip through the maze visibly upset. She stomped up to Stacy and hissed, "One of your actors called me a bitch."

Stacy peered behind the woman. There were no actors posted in the section of the maze she had just left. "Ma'am ... there's no one in there."

"No," the woman insisted, "one of your actors tapped me on the shoulder and called me a bitch."

Stacy knew her charges better than that. She knew that whoever had insulted the woman was someone who was long past being reprimanded for their rudeness.

*Elisabeth*

Along with the Men's Ward, one of the most active areas of the Pollak Hospital is the basement. The Pollak was the site of many deaths through the years – at times, the death toll reached three to five deaths a week. When a patient died, the body was brought down to the basement and put into cold storage. From there, the deceased would either be claimed by his or her family for burial in a family plot, or they'd be buried in one of the cemeteries at the asylum. The basement of the Pollak holds a cool chill even in the hottest days of summer.

Paranormal investigators who venture down here are treated to a wealth of experiences. I myself have been skunked good by the spirits down there. One night I was at the Pollak with Peoria Paranormal. We began the evening's investigation in the basement, then left to explore another part of the building. There were eight of us or so, and we all headed for the basement steps. I've got this thing where I don't like to be the last person out of a dark, haunted room, so I made absolutely sure there was someone behind me as we went up the stairs. It was dark and we had only flashlights, but I saw enough to know that there was a girl wearing a puffy blue ski jacket behind me on the stairs. I even held the door at the top of the stairs for her – but when I turned around to hold it, I was in fact the last one in line. My stomach gave a nasty lurch when I saw the empty stairs leading back down into the darkness.

Keith Hasdall, of Central Illinois Ghost Investigators, has actually been chased up the basement stairs by some unseen phantom. He was doing an investigation in the basement when he felt an eerie presence behind him. Deciding he'd had enough of the basement for a while, he headed up the stairs. About halfway up, something pushed him from behind, as if to hurry him the rest of the way.

There are several entities in the basement, each with their own distinct personality. There is a big, gruff guy with a chip on his shoulder the size of Old Book's Graveyard Elm. He's a nasty, belligerent spirit with a foul temper and an even fouler mouth. There are some investigators he hates more than others. Derek Waldschmidt, of Peoria Paranormal, seems to be pretty high up on this guy's shit list. Whenever Derek is in the basement with the ghost box running, "Seth" is sure to turn up and turn the air blue. (Chris doesn't like to speak his name aloud down in the basement. She feels it gives him more power and energy every time his name is mentioned.)

This entity likes to throw his ectoplasmic weight around. Jackie, Mindy, and Erin, volunteers at the Pollak, have all felt his bullying presence in the basement. Mindy felt a tightness in her shoulder. Jackie felt pain in the back of her neck – Erin felt it too. Jackie said it felt like someone pressing a hot poker against the muscles of her neck. It didn't ease until she moved, or until "Seth" relented and let her go.

Stacy, the sensitive, has asked this angry spirit why he hurts people who venture into the basement. The answer? *"Because I can."* This entity considers the basement his turf. When he's on the scene, the ghost box will repeatedly spit out the word *"angry"*. He'll also invite male investigators, particularly Derek, to *"suck my dick"*. "Seth" is a nasty character, no question about it.

Another entity that makes the basement her home is the spirit of a young girl. Sensitives say her name is "Elizabeth". Investigators think she's about five years old, and that she may have had a speech impediment in life. Most of the EVPs that can be attributed to her come out garbled, as though she has trouble speaking.

But even if Elizabeth can't speak very well, she has no problem communicating. She is a playful, lively spirit. When Illinois Ghost Seekers Society did an investigation at the Pollak, several of the ghost hunters were sitting in the basement when a small pebble came flying at them, thrown by an invisible hand. Moments later, a ghostly giggle floated up on the recording.

The volunteers at the Pollak are fond of their little prankster ghost. They've left a small teddy bear and an old-fashioned doll in the basement as playtoys for Elizabeth. And play she does. As an experiment, a volunteer once left the doll sitting on the concrete floor. All around the doll, the volunteer sprinkled a circle of baby powder. The next time someone came down to the basement, the doll was lying on her side – and there was a perfect circle in the sprinkling of baby powder, the drag marks of the doll's fabric heels as it was spun around on the floor.

Elizabeth seems to enjoy having visitors. One of our investigations in the basement turned out to be quite eventful for Sam Callear. He was down there with several other ghost hunters – I was with the group that evening too – when he felt a gentle tug on his arm.

"I feel something on my arm, pulling it down," he reported. Sam's very good at telling the rest of the group whenever he sees or feels something out of the ordinary.

"Tell it thank you," Stacy suggested. She was holding a K-II meter, and when Sam called out, "Thank you," the meter flashed and beeped.

"She likes to play with the lights," Stacy explained.

"My jacket!" Sam blurted. We looked over at him, and everyone gasped. Sam was wearing an athletic jacket, which was hanging open, unzipped. As we all watched, the edges of the jacket moved, as though small hands were grasping it.

"Oh my God, oh my God, it's scary," Sam panted.

"Sam, it's okay. They like you, Sam, it's okay."

A short shadow moved to stand in front of the nervous teenager.

"*Don't move,* Sam. Guys, watch the front of his coat, it's moving again."

"My heart's racing," Sam moaned, but he stood his ground.

"Take a deep breath, Sam," we encouraged him. The kid was amazing. He was obviously terrified by this brush with the unknown, but his nerve never broke, not once. The shadow soon moved away, and the edges of Sam's jacket hung limply in front of him. Sam's shoulders slumped as he let out the breath he'd been holding. A grin split his face ear to ear.

"Oh my gosh, that was *awesome!*" (Stacy mentioned this experience during her appearance in Living Dead Paranormal's The Asylum Project film. It's at the beginning of the film, during the first five minutes.)

Elizabeth wasn't finished with us yet. Sam is very good at asking questions that are easily answered. "Are you scared? Can you knock and tell us how old you are? Are there others here with you? Can you knock how many people are here with you?" At one point, he asked, "Do you miss your mom?", and the K-II meter spiked.

"I've never seen these things go off like this down here," another investigator said.

The air was cool, but Stacy said that ghost hunters have had the experience of being drenched in sweat in the basement, even in the dead of winter.

"It was just ... *heat,* I couldn't explain it. And it was just as cold out as it is now."

Sam jumped in spite of himself. "Felt like someone grabbed my hand," he apologized. Then a look of wonder spread over his face.

"Oh, it's really warm!"

This is pure conjecture, of course, but we like to think that Sam reminds Elizabeth of a long-lost big brother. She held his hand for five minutes or so. Then Sam reported that the warm feeling faded.

*"Dork."*

Most of the energy in the Pollak is comfortable, gentle, even playful. One Friday night, several investigators were sitting in one of the few furnished rooms at the hospital, sprawled on the two couches, having fun with a ghost box.

"Can you tell us the names of everybody in this room?"

The ghost box made its way around the room. *"Trudi." "Stacy."* *"Jackie."* When it was Dustin's turn, the ghost box hesitated.

"Come on, what's his name?" they prompted.

The ghost box chuckled, *"Dork."*

Stacy likes to think that this playfulness shows that there are intelligent spirits in the place, ghosts with a sense of humor. On another occasion, the investigators asked, "How many spirits live here?" The ghost box shot back, *"Too many."*

The Pollak is sometimes used by filmmakers in search of a suitable atmospheric setting for a creepy movie. During the summer of 2012, a crew was shooting a zombie movie at the building. Actors were shambling around in the basement, doing the classic *"step-draaggg, step-draaggg"* shuffle of the living dead. The director yelled "Cut!", and the actors relaxed.

Then, from the empty upstairs hallway, the people in the basement heard an unmistakable *"step-draaggg, step-draaggg"* – as if something upstairs was mimicking their performance.

Chris told me that spirits can also follow visitors home. "We've had people come back and tell us that on the way home, their car radio went on by itself, and the passenger seat reclined with no one in it. They'll get home, and the spirits will open kitchen cabinets and spill food all over the floor. These people will come back here and say, 'Look, could you please take these ghosts back?' We just tell them, the spirits are looking for a home. They just chose to go home with you this time. Of course, we always welcome our ghosts back."

The spirits at the Pollak seem to have their favorites, too. A medium visiting the building turned to Chris during her tour and said, "By the way, the spirits want to tell you to thank Cathe for coming out to help."

Chris realized immediately whom the medium was referring to – her mother, who comes to the Pollak often to help with the haunt.

One summer day, Chris and Jill were at the building, and Chris needed to call her mom. Cathe was planning to come to the building later that day. Chris dialed her cell phone, expecting to be connected with her mom.

Cathe answered her phone, but heard only heavy, gasping breathing, as if someone was desperately fighting for air.

Chris hung up and tried again. This time, Cathe heard only indistinct whispering on her end of the connection.

Frustrated with shouting, "Hello? Hello!?", Chris tried one more time to connect. On her end, Cathe heard only the *click* of someone ending the call.

Later that evening, Cathe showed up as she'd promised. She's a neat freak, according to Chris, so the first thing she did was to go into one of the exam rooms, flip the light switch on, and start picking up clutter. Chris and Jill were walking down the hall and passed the room where Cathe was working. Jill slid to an astonished stop on the linoleum floor. Behind her, Chris said, "What? What?" in concern. Her next *"Whaaat?!?"* was a bray of disbelief as she looked into the room.

"We were like dogs doing that head-tilt thing," Chris told me. "I said, 'Mom, what are you doing?'"

Calmly, Cathe replied, "I'm cleaning."

That's when Chris and Jill told Cathe that the lights in that room hadn't worked since the haunt that past October ... five months previously.

## Other Experiences

A woman who was walking around behind the Pollak Building heard the sound of children playing under one of the trees, even though there was no one there. She pointed her camera at the tree anyway, and snapped a picture. The picture later showed two children happily engrossed in playing some game around the base of the tree and in its branches.

Sharon Wood was at the Pollak Hospital late one October night while the Haunted Infirmary was going on. She was walking around the outside of the building, and felt drawn to take a picture of the tree behind the building. When she looked at the picture later, she noticed what appeared to be puffy, cartoon-like letters in amongst the leaves and branches.

The letters were "TB".

(This is known in the paranormal field as "ghost writing". Words show up in photographs, words that weren't there when the picture was taken. Is this an example of matrixing, the human mind's drive to impose sense on the unfamiliar? Or is it a message from the beyond?)

An investigator with SPIRIT went through the Haunted Infirmary one October. He had a cut on his leg, but since it was covered by his jeans, he didn't tell his friends about it. He was unnerved to feel an insistent tapping on his leg while he was going through the haunt, precisely at the spot where he'd been cut. Later, he felt an icy-cold grip on his finger. He asked the empty room: "Are you here with anybody?"

A single knock came in reply.

The ghost hunter asked, "How many spirits are here with you?"

The answering barrage of knocks was continuous – too many to count.

Judy Sullivan was visiting the Pollak with her mother, Dorothy, who is sensitive, and a friend, Larry. Larry was taping as they walked along, and excitedly said, "There are bunches of kids around here!" Dorothy, who can see spirits, assured the group, "We're surrounded by kids right now."

Larry was fiddling with the recorder, when he looked up, excitement dancing in his eyes, and yelled, "Judy, you have to listen to this!" He held up the recorder.

On the recording, Larry muttered to himself, "Did I just hear a tap-tap-tap on the window?"

In reply, a child's voice piped up, *"Yup, you sure did!"*

Chris, of course, has many stories to tell about her experiences at the Pollak. Once, Chris was walking down the main hallway when she saw a woman's leg, clad in a skirt, coming through the door. Not through the doorway – through the *door*. Chris called for Cathe, her mom, to come and watch, but the spirit didn't manifest any further. As the two women watched, the skirt faded away.

Another time, Chris was in the building when a little girl asked a question behind her. The words were unintelligible, but the inflection was definitely that of a question. Chris thought that maybe a volunteer was on the other side of the window and had asked her something, but when she went to investigate, there was no one there.

## A Legacy of Caring

The Pollak Hospital is another haven for spirits on the hilltop. So many people passed from this life in the building that it is, of course, a ghostly hotspot. That in itself would practically guarantee paranormal activity.

But as we've seen, there is another aspect to the hospital, another facet that mirrors the entire philosophy of this asylum. The Pollak Hospital was a place of caring that opened its doors to the community. The doctors and nurses at the asylum saw a need in the surrounding area for a hospital that would treat tuberculosis patients regardless of their ability to pay. The staff took in TB sufferers from the community, as well as patients at the asylum. Everyone found help here, not only the insane.

I'm pleased to say that the present "staff" of the Pollak Hospital continues this legacy of caring for the less fortunate. One spring day, Jeff, one of the volunteers, heard strange scratchy noises in the wall of the building – noises that didn't seem to have their origin on the Other Side. An investigation revealed a nest of baby raccoons. Their mother had moved them from a previous nesting space, then had gotten separated from her kits. Jeff rescued the babies and got them set up in a cozy nesting box with blankets in one of the office. A space heater provided soothing warmth. Stacy and the other volunteers took turns feeding the baby raccoons kitten formula every couple of hours. (To my intense delight, I got to help. I'm a sucker for baby animals, and these raccoon kits were adorrrrable.)

I think Dr. Zeller would approve.

# OTHER BUILDINGS

Of the sixty-five original buildings of the Peoria State Hospital, there are only thirteen left. Out of the four hospitals of the asylum, only the Pollak remains. The Leviton, the Talcott, The Rose Bigler, many of the cottages, they're all gone now. Pfeiffer Road was put through in the 1980s. The Talcott Building was razed to accommodate the construction of the road. Pfeiffer Road, at the bottom of the hill, actually cuts through what would have been the basements of the Talcott Building and one wing of the Zeller Building. It's no wonder people have reported seeing "white figures" in the road. They're driving through the nonexistent basements of two buildings.

Many of the remaining buildings are former dormitories. They have open floor plans, as opposed to the cottages, which were more like spacious homes. Many of the cottages were demolished after the asylum closed, as they were not suited for conversion to either industrial or business use. The dorms, though, with their open floor plans, are still in use today by local businesses.

The Bowen is the grand old lady of the Peoria State Hospital. The Pollak is the hidden haunted gem. But there are several other buildings on the hilltop that are worth our attention. Some of them are now gone, although many still stand.

And all of them are haunted.

*Stone Country*

Stone Country Saloon, to use its full name, is an all ages country dance club that sits sort of at the third point of a rough triangle, with the other two points being the Bowen Building and the Pollak Hospital. If you walk up to the door of Stone Country after six pm on a Wednesday, Thursday, Friday, or Saturday night, you'll hear the thump of country dance music beyond the door. And if you go inside, you'll find yourself in a large, open space, bright with lights, happy with the beat of country music, and alive with the stomp and clap of line dancers enjoying that music.

There's plenty of room at the bar to dance, because this building used to be the gymnasium for the Peoria State Hospital. The ceilings are high enough to accommodate even the most energetic game of basketball, and the polished wood floors still squeak under the quick turn of a gym shoe.

It's no secret that Stone Country is haunted. Dan Stone bought the building in 1995, and opened Stone Country Saloon soon afterwards. The gymnasium was young, compared to the other buildings on the hilltop; it was built in 1963, only ten years before the asylum closed. But that was long enough for spirits to get attached to the place.

GUARD (Ghost Unit Analysis Research and Detection) investigated Stone Country in December 2009. They came away with several interesting EVPs, which can be found on their website. These ghost voices include the sound of someone whistling, and an extremely faint voice insisting *"Let me say something"*.

However, it's the employees that are the real experts on the hauntings at Stone Country. Karl Nash, a part time employee at the bar, told me that Michael, the deejay, won't go into the building without someone to go with him. "And he's three times my size," Karl guffaws.

It was Karl's fiancée, Arin, who shared a barrage of stories with me.

"I always got a creepy feeling in that building anyway. I never felt comfortable being alone in there, even before my first experience.

"I said, 'If you're here, I want to see it.' I don't know what I was thinking – I guess I just wanted to get it over with. Right after I said that, I walked down the length of the bar. When I was halfway down, a dimmer switch flew off of the wall and hit me in the shoulder. I said, 'Okay, I'm sorry, I won't doubt you again.' What's weird is that after that, I seemed to get more sensitive.

"I was at the bar once and I heard someone whistle a tune right in my ear. It was a melody I'd never heard before. I turned my head, and I felt someone brush my hair away from my face." She shuddered. "I'm getting goosebumps telling you about it now," she said with a grimace.

"There are TV screens in the bar. Sometimes, when the televisions are off but the lights in the bar are on, you can see a reflection in the screen of people walking behind you. But when you turn around to look, they're not there.

"Mikey [the deejay] was turning on the lights by the pool table one afternoon when we were getting ready to open. He felt a piece of pool chalk hit him. His wife happened to be near him, so he turned to her and said, 'Why did you throw that at me – why are you being mean?' His wife shot back, 'I don't know what you're talking about.' Mike looked down at his shirt, and he could see the mark left by the pool chalk.

"Another employee, Kamisha, left her ball cap on the bar while she went to turn the lights on in the men's room. When she came back out, seconds later, the cap was in the middle of the dance floor.

"After closing, we sometimes just hang out at the bar. We can hear barstools moving around upstairs, in the loft area above the bar. We'll go up and straighten all the barstools, and then we'll go back downstairs. Then we'll hear the stools moving around again." She shrugged.

"There's really nothing we can do about it."

## The Cottages

The cottages were what set the Peoria State Hospital apart from many other asylums in the United States. During the nineteenth and early twentieth century, many asylums were built on the Kirkbride plan, named after the architect who designed it. This plan called for one large octagonal building as the hub, with four wings coming out from the central building. These wings could be expanded indefinitely, according to the housing needs of the asylum. The original building of the Peoria State Hospital (then known as the Illinois Asylum for the Incurable Insane) was actually built on the Kirkbride plan. It was also built on an abandoned coal mine, out of shoddy materials, by contractors that were rumored to have ties to the Chicago Mob. Dr. Zeller refused to use the building. In 1898, having never actually housed any patients, the building was deemed unfit for habitation, and was torn down. The limestone blocks were soon used to build the Bowen.

In the Kirkbride plan, all of the asylum's patients were housed in one building, without regard for their afflictions. Someone who was merely depressed could have a paranoid schizophrenic as a roommate – not the ideal situation for improving mental health.

In the cottage plan, people with similar issues were housed together. Epileptics were paired off in a buddy system in case of fits. Alcoholics helped each other through the agony of withdrawal. All of the patients lived in cottages, which were managed by a married couple – sort of a "house mom" and "dad". This gave the patients the needed illusion of home.

Over the years since the asylum's closing, it became obvious that the spirits still considered the cottages to be home. And no wonder – when the asylum closed, the cottages were just left exactly as they were. Furniture, tables, plates, pianos warped out of tune – all relics of a place some people simply wanted to forget.

A man I spoke to (who asked that his name not be used) told me that one afternoon, before most of the cottages were torn down, he and his wife were taking a walk through the streets of Bartonville. As they passed one of the cottages, they heard piano music coming from inside, a simple, tuneful melody. They walked in through the open front door, but no one was inside. The piano they had heard still stood in the dayroom, its keys broken, its top warped.

The man and his wife left, chills chasing each other down their spines. When they reached the safety of the sidewalk, they heard the notes of the piano again. They turned to look through the big front window of the cottage, and saw a little girl with long straight hair standing next to the piano.

"We thought about calling out to her," the man told me, "until we realized she wasn't really there."

## The Angel of God

Across Constitution Drive from the Bowen Building is an empty lot, barren except for the weeds poking up through cracks in the concrete. The plant life of central Illinois, the lamb's quarters and the dandelions and the common bindweed and the quackgrass, is quickly reclaiming this small piece of the hilltop. This empty lot is where the Domestic Building once stood, a complex of structures including the employees' dining hall, the bakery, the kitchen, and the Industrial Building. The dining hall was badly damaged in a fire in 1964. By that time, patients and staff alike were using the cottages as dining facilities, so the employees' dining hall was not rebuilt after the fire. After the asylum's closing in 1973, all of the buildings suffered badly from exposure to the elements. The complex was finally demolished a few years ago, in 2009.

The Domestic Building was the source of a strong sense of creep before it was torn down, and with very good reason. The Industrial Building served as the laundry facility for the hilltop. On the second floor of the building was a powerful, dangerous machine that pressed and folded sheets. It's commonly referred to as a "mangler", and it comes by the gruesome nickname honestly. Two workers suffered frightful injuries when they were sucked into the mangler and their arms were crushed. They were lucky to escape with their lives. Another worker wasn't so fortunate. A moment's careless inattention, and he was pulled into the mangler. His head was pulped, and he died instantly.

Two more deaths occurred in an accident when two men fell down an elevator shaft. One of the men died on impact; the other died later in the hospital. Chris Morris captured a chilling EVP that may reflect the men's last moments. In a recording made near the elevator shaft, a man's voice can be heard saying something about "hanging on".

It was the Dining Hall that was the scene of one of the most infamous deaths at the Peoria State Hospital. In December 1966, a patient named James Sample was working in the kitchen, helping with food preparation. Sample suffered under the delusion that he was the "Angel of God". He kept the "staff of God" tucked under his arm at all times. (According to the newspaper article about the incident, this was a metal pry bar, used for removing milk can lids. A gentle tapping with the end of the bar all around the can's lid breaks the seal, and the lid can be easily pried off.)

Sample was going about his kitchen duties with the metal rod tucked securely under his arm. A cook saw him working one-handed. She said, "Use both hands," and took the rod from under his arm and put it on the table.

"I am the Angel of God! You do NOT touch the Staff!" Sample roared. He snatched up the "Staff" and smote the unbeliever. The first blow split her skull nearly in half. He rained down punishment, lashing out in a berserk rage, swinging his weapon at anyone who dared to come close. (By this time, he may have thought he was defending himself against the orderlies who were piling onto him to stop his rampage.) The incident ended with one woman dead, and three nurses injured.

This tragedy, along with the deaths in the Industrial Building, left an indelible psychic imprint on the area. The details may differ in the telling, but stories are still whispered about the woman who was killed in the Dining Hall. The story above is what was reported in the local newspaper. This is the most accurate account of the incident I could pick out of the many versions I heard.

While doing the research for this book, I met a woman named Jamee Congrove. She's a sensitive, and so is her six year old son. "He takes walks through the cemeteries with me," she told me. "It doesn't bother him to see ghosts. Sometimes the energy is very sad, as though the spirits don't want to be there. But other times, the ghosts will just run up to you – they're so happy that people are there to visit them."

About ten years ago, Jamee was in the Dining Hall. She was exploring, as so many adventurers have done before her. It was there that she felt a physical blow to the back of her head, at the very same place the cook was bludgeoned with the Staff of God.

## The Phoenix Club

If you follow an investigation long enough, there will be times, even in the most promising of circumstances, that you'll come to a dead end. This happened to me in the middle of the wealth of paranormal occurrences that swirl around the hilltop.

The building that now houses the Phoenix Club used to be part of the entertainment complex for the asylum. The Phoenix Club sits right next to Stone Country. On the night I visited, I was feeling pretty good. I had spent the afternoon tromping through the woods exploring the ravines behind the cemeteries. I had seen the curious stone carvings on the rock face in the ravine. I had just come from Stone Country, where I'd spent nearly an hour listening to a fellow ghost hunter spin tales of the hauntings he'd investigated. I was hoping, as I pulled open the door and walked into the restaurant, to make it three for three, to wrap up the evening with another round of stories.

That plan fizzled.

I strolled up to the bar. An older guy in a red t-shirt sat behind the bar, his back to me, his attention captured by the NASCAR race on the television mounted near the ceiling. He sat watching the race silently, while a customer at the end of the bar provided a loud running commentary.

The waitress, a short woman who looked vaguely Asian, came up to me. "Can I help you?"

I introduced myself. "I understand the Phoenix Club used to be one of the buildings of the old asylum, and I was wondering if there was anyone here who could tell me a few good ghost stories." I smiled. *See? I really am harmless.*

The older man in the red t-shirt shifted on his stool. The waitress shook her head and spoke in a firm voice. "I'm a Christian. I don't believe in those ghosts."

The chatty guy at the end of the bar piped up – he must have heard me over the roar of the NASCAR. "Hey, we've got ghost stories. Ask him, he'll tell ya." He pointed at the older man. "I don't know how much he's had to drink, but he's seen 'em, as stupid as that sounds." He swung himself off of his barstool, grinned, tapped a cigarette out of a pack, and headed out the door to have a smoke.

The man in the red t-shirt got up and walked unhurriedly to the kitchen door at the far end of the bar. I was torn – should I wait for him to come back out? Should I follow the talkative guy outside and pump him for more details?

After several minutes of pretending to be interested in the sports memorabilia that hung on the walls, I realized that the guy in the red t-shirt hadn't yet emerged from the kitchen. Either the NASCAR race wasn't exciting enough to hold his interest, or he was avoiding me. I went back up to the bar, where the waitress was wiping the counter.

"So … that other fellow said –"

"Has Brad been telling you stories?" she snapped.

"Well, he said the guy in the red shirt had seen something – but it doesn't seem like he wants to talk to me." I offered her a smile, but she wasn't buying.

"No, no, that's my husband. We don't believe in ghosts," she repeated firmly. If she had requested that I not allow the door to hit me on the ass on my way out, I wouldn't have been surprised.

*The Octagon Building*

The Octagon Building, just a few blocks away from the Bowen Building, was originally the doctors' library. Eventually, it became a common area for the patients. It functioned as a commissary, a beauty shop, a barber shop, and a shoe repair shop.

Every single building on the hilltop had a round window built into it somewhere, a nod to an ancient architectural superstition that a round window would keep away evil spirits. In the Octagon Building, this was the round skylight, which still exists today, even after its remodel.

One might be tempted to question the efficacy of that superstition. There have been several spirits identified in the Octagon Building. One of them, according to several paranormal groups that have investigated the place, is the ghost of a criminally insane sexual deviant. (So much for round windows keeping nasty ghosts away.) The investigators identified this particular spirit as a troublemaker, and said (perhaps unnecessarily) that it doesn't like women intruding on its territory. It may have been this entity that called Chris Morris "*a fucking bitch*".

Bu that's not the only spirit that calls the Octagon Building home. Stacy Carroll was there with her son Ricky. As they recorded, they picked up a female voice cooing, "*Don't leave me, cutie*". (Ghost hunters have identified two female spirits in the building, in addition to the "troublemaker". As of this writing, investigators claimed to have helped the two female spirits pass over. The angry male spirit, though, refused to move on.)

Jennifer Hartley shared an experience her husband, Chad, had in the building. "A group of ghost hunters was in the building for the night, so Chad and I had to be there. At one point, just because I needed something to do, I cleaned off his desk. I threw away several water bottles and soda cans. I threw them away in a garbage can on the opposite side of the building from Chad's office. His office door is always locked, and no one else has keys.

"When he returned to the building on Monday, Chad called me. 'You threw all that stuff on my desk away, didn't you?' I said that yeah, I did. That's when he told me that four of the empty soda cans were back on his desk, stacked in a neat pile.

"Chad's a complete nonbeliever, but even he says that the building had weird stuff going on. Keys, tools, equipment … it would either get moved when no one was looking, or it would just disappear. He also said that when his company moved out of the building to a new office, employees (including Chad himself) said that they felt happier, less anxious, 'as if a weight had been lifted off their shoulders'. This new office was less than a block away from the Octagon Building, but that short distance made all the difference."

# CEMETERIES AND RAVINES

*"The longer you sit there, picking through the artifacts, the spookier and spookier it gets." -- Chris Morris*

The cemeteries of the asylum are, naturally, a rich source of stories and experiences. Unlike the buildings of the asylum, the cemeteries, and the ravines that cut through the bluff top, are open to anyone who wants to explore them.

And people do explore them. Some go just for the thrill of poking around in a cemetery. There's a fair amount of vandalism, unfortunately. The volunteers at the buildings often find tombstones down in the ravines – but the stones don't end up there from washouts or heavy rains.

"Kids like to steal the headstones," Chris Morris explained. "Since the stones are all numbered, any stone with a '13' in the number is particularly popular. They pry the headstone up and start to make their getaway through the ravine, where no one will see them carrying it. Then they discover, about halfway through, that it's damn heavy to lug a headstone around. They decide 'this sucks', and they just drop it."

Visitors often ask why many of the stones simply have numbers rather than names. Some of the stones do have names, particularly the stones in Cemetery 1, where the patients of well-to-do families were buried.

But many are simply marked with the patient's ID number. Illinois state law only provides for grave markers to bear names if that name is legally accepted – it can only be on your gravestone if it's also on your birth certificate. Since many of the patients were known by nicknames, or were physically unable to communicate their legal name to the intake nurses, Dr. Zeller decided that patients would be buried using their identification number. Dr. Zeller also believed in equality for all. He felt that by using numbers rather than names on the stones, the asylum could preserve the patients' anonymity. The hospital kept records of who was buried where. Unfortunately, all those records were lost when the hospital closed.

The hoopla surrounding Old Book's funeral bothered Doc Zeller quite a bit. He felt that none of his patients should be found more interesting, even in death, than any of the others. In spite of this, Old Book's gravesite is now marked with a plaque. People leave trinkets there – Mardi Gras beads, coins, lighters (perhaps in a nod to the failed attempt to burn down the dying Graveyard Elm), and, oddly enough, books.

(This is a puzzling thing. If someone was a bookbinder by trade, and went insane due to the pressures of work … the very last thing you'd think they'd want on their grave would be offerings of books.)

Families that could afford the expense provided headstones for their loved ones. Other patients were simply acknowledged with their number. All of them sleep under the Illinois soil, equal now in the most basic, final way of all.

*The Cemeteries*

Over the years of the asylum's operation, from 1902 to 1973, 4132 patients were buried in the hospital grounds. Many more patients than this actually died here, though. This number does not include patients whose bodies were claimed by their families for burial elsewhere.

Depending on who is doing the counting, there are anywhere from three to five cemeteries on the grounds of the asylum. Some people consider the GAR cemetery to be its own burying ground, and honestly, it is. But for simplicity's sake, we'll consider it to be part of Cemetery 1. Cemetery 2 is its own little pocket of greenery, so no one ever disputes it. Cemetery 3 is sometimes divided into two parts, simply because of the road that runs through it. Again, to keep things simple, we'll just call that Cemetery 3.

Whether there are five cemeteries or three, they all have their own distinct feel. Cemetery 1 is located along South Becker Drive. The energy here is peaceful. There are 326 gravestones here. Nearly every grave is decorated with flowers, and every grave in the veterans' section has an American flag standing at attention before the headstone. The "soldier known only to God" has a flag as well.

This cemetery contains the graves of those patients whose families were well off, who could afford a nicer headstone and upkeep on a gravesite. Rhoda Derry is buried here, in the oldest cemetery on the hilltop. Like Bookbinder's grave, her headstone is marked with a plaque bearing a remembrance of her importance to the asylum's history. And as with Bookbinder's grave, people leave mementos – coins, rosaries, little tokens of their affection for this unfortunate woman whose amazing story is still remembered today.

The energy at Cemetery 2 is more secretive, a little bit wilder. Cemetery 2 is just steps away from the front door of the Pollak Hospital, down a short swale that opens up into a secret expanse of green. This graveyard is surrounded by underbrush and tall, tall trees, giving it the air of being hidden away from the curious. Old Book is one of 532 patients buried in this graveyard. The patients here were all buried in the fetal position to save on space. This explains why the headstones in the cemeteries are spaced so closely together.

Cemetery 3 (or Cemeteries 3 and 4) is the one that feels most like a modern graveyard. And it does contain the most recent burials, including the last burial on the hilltop. George Krasousky, aged 84, died on August 6, 1973. The last eighteen patients at the Peoria State Hospital left for their new home at the Galesburg State Research Hospital on December 18, 1973.

Cemetery 3 has 1842 graves, and Cemetery 4 has 901 graves. The two cemeteries are separated (or the one large graveyard is bisected) by a long, paved road called "The Glory Walk" or "The Pathway to Heaven". This wide, flat promenade down the center of the graveyard reflects cemetery design of the 1920s.

As in the first two cemeteries, there is a gravesite that is worth mentioning in Cemetery 3. Emily Belcher is buried here. She was a member of some European royal family. When she was diagnosed with her troubles, her family searched the world for the institution that would provide the very best care for her. Out of all the sanitariums world-wide, they chose the Peoria State Hospital. She was committed, and spent many years living here, quite content. Every month, her family sent her a "care package" – a pound of silver, to provide for her upkeep.

During her final illness, Emily wrote to her family. She said, "I know that I'm dying, and that I should be buried in my homeland. But this is now my home. These people are now my family. I would like to be buried here, on the grounds of the Peoria State Hospital, in a place where I feel comfortable and accepted." Her family agreed to follow her wishes. Emily is now buried with her adopted "family" in Cemetery 3.

Mattie Sutton is one of the volunteers working to replace missing stones at the cemeteries, and the stones that have started to buckle and sink into the soil due to the heaves of frost and thaw of decades of Illinois winters. She is a student of mortuary science, and she has taken the cemeteries of the Peoria State Hospital under her wing. Many of the headstones are crumbling, and others are sinking into the ground. The process is simple, honest work: a volunteer spades a stone out of the clinging ground, levering it from the earth's embrace. Then he fills the hole with several inches of soil, bringing the dirt up to its original level. He wrestles the stone back into place, and checks its position with a level. Then it's on to the next stone, and the next, and the next...

Sutton's interest in the cemeteries goes back to her teen years, when she first heard about the asylum. She would go to the cemeteries in the daytime, just to sit and think in the tranquil silence.

"Who bothers you when you're in a cemetery?" She realized then the true purpose of the graveyards: "Zeller wanted people to come out here to be able to mourn."

Sutton is doing her best to assist people with that. There are still plenty of people in the area who had relatives at the asylum, relatives who are buried on the grounds. Through Sutton's research, people have found the graves of their relatives, gravesites once thought to be lost. Recalling that sense of history and connection is Sutton's purpose. That, and restoring the cemeteries to their original dignified, reflective state.

*"You want to know what's funny?"*

Gary Lisman, author of *Bittersweet Memories: A History of the Peoria State Hospital,* lives in Bartonville. Every evening, he walks his dog along the quiet streets. The circuit takes him past the cemeteries. The dog enjoys her nightly stroll ... but she refuses to cut through the cemeteries.

Sharon Wood, one of the Bowen Building volunteers, was visiting the large cemetery at night with a tour group. As so often happens, some of the teenagers in the group were behaving badly, getting rowdy and disrespectful. Sharon frowned. She knew that her daughter, and her daughter's friend, would never behave so poorly in a cemetery.

Suddenly her daughter's friend yelped. "Someone just pinched me!" The girl later discovered that she'd been scratched as well.

Still upset by the disrespectful teenagers, Sharon tried to leave the cemetery and take the nervous girls with her. That's when she realized that something invisible was standing on her feet.

"I couldn't move," she says. "I was trying, trying to move my feet so we could leave, but I couldn't move."

Candi Nearing Mastronardi is another volunteer at the Bowen Building. One warm fall evening during a Creepy Campout, she had been assigned to stand near Cemetery 1 to act as a guide for any campers who happened to wander past. She was at her post, standing next to the GAR cemetery, all alone in the darkness, when she heard the "tramp, tramp, tramp" of invisible booted feet marching past her on the road.

Chris Morris and Stacy Carroll have worked with several ghost hunting groups in the cemeteries. They've collected some amazing EVPs along the way. When Peoria Paranormal was recording in one of the cemeteries, Derek asked aloud, "Do you want to cross over?" Shortly after that, a man's voice replied, *"No."* Then a woman chimed in: *"No."*

Stacy spoke next. "Do you want to go into the light? It's beautiful."

A man's stern voice replied, *"Liar."* Apparently he had his own opinions about the Light.

In June of 2011, I went to one of the Creepy Campouts. As usual, groups went to explore after dark in the cemeteries. I went with a group to Cemetery 2, where Bookbinder is buried. The woods loomed black all around the graveyard. Trees moved restlessly in the night breeze. Cicadas were singing loudly in the warm darkness, making recording nearly impossible. I soon gave up on capturing any EVPs, and decide to enjoy the electric atmosphere of the warm summer evening. Nerves were wound tight with the thrill of exploring a haunted graveyard in the middle of the night. People paced the graveyard, cameras at the ready, alert for any movement in the shadows among the gravestones.

A teenage volunteer rushed up to me and grabbed my hand. She was shaking with terror, and her eyes were wide with shock.

"In the woods – I just saw a face!" she stammered. "I was over there, by the ravine, and I looked into the trees and I saw a face! It was crying – I think I might have seen Old Book!"

Was this the power of suggestion working on a susceptible teenage girl, someone who was already wound up with the excitement of a ghost hunt? Did her mind conjure a screaming face out of shifting shadows? Her terror was real, I can guarantee you that.

AJ Rodgers is a medium who has been exploring the asylum for many years. Intense, with tattoos and black spiky hair, he's about as far away from the conventional picture of a medium as you can get. But his intensity comes from hard-won experience. He's a ghost hunter who gets out in the field, and he's got the stories to prove it.

AJ was out at Cemetery 1 when he had his first encounter with a spirit he calls "The Guardian". AJ was walking towards the cemetery, fully intending to explore, when he became aware of a black mass undulating above the headstones. He described it as a "hot spot".

"Before I stepped into the cemetery, he was basically letting me know, you're not coming in here, not tonight. When something takes a step towards me, and that step is fifteen feet …"

It was September 2, 2011. A harvest moon hung low and fiery in the sky, a glow of orange and red. AJ was at the cemetery with his ghost hunting group. A Bartonville police officer pulled up to see what the group was doing there. AJ was recording, and he let the recorder run as he stood next to the police car, speaking with the officer.

As they spoke, AJ had a gut feeling that something significant had just been picked up on the recorder. Holding up a finger, he paused in his conversation with the officer. He hit the rewind button, waited a few moments, then pressed PLAY.

A dark, deep, frightening voice boomed out of the small machine. *"AJ, tell your mom I'm coming for her."*

The police officer jumped, startled. "What the hell was that?"

"That was someone standing right next to you," AJ replied.

The officer backed towards the safety of his car. "Don't vandalize anything," he warned, pointing at the group. He opened his car door and swung himself behind the wheel. "I'll be back in an hour to make sure you're still alive."

Shane Cleer, of SPIRIT (Shane's Paranormal Investigative Research Intelligence Team – their motto, "If you fear it, just call SPIRIT"), claims to have had a spectacular experience in one of the cemeteries. He was in Cemetery 3 with his team using a ghost box to communicate with the spirits. He asked, "Do you like me?" The ghost box responded, *"No."* He pressed: "Do you want to fight?"

*"Yes."*

One of his ghost hunters moaned, "Oh, I feel sick. I'm getting all cold and clammy, like there's an ice pack on the back of my neck." That same investigator ended up vomiting three times. A female investigator heard the sound of someone sniffling – not crying, just sobbing quietly. She also felt a pressure on her skull, as though her head was about to explode. It messed with her perception so badly that for a few minutes, she "forgot" how to walk. It took conscious effort for her just to put one foot in front of the other to make her way out of the cemetery.

William "Bill" Turner is a former employee of the Peoria State Hospital. During his employment there, he would take boys from the adolescent ward out camping. One summer night, he and his assistant were taking the boys out for a "star hike" to do some stargazing. Their hike took them past Cemetery 4. The boys swore they saw a dark shadow floating in the cemetery, a shadow which drifted off into the trees when they approached.

Rob Conover regularly takes groups out to the cemeteries for tours. On one occasion he escorted several radio personalities from the Morning Mix out to the back part of Cemetery 3. A young photographer took along her infrared camera. In the cemetery, Rob met the spirit of an old man, and struck up a conversation with him. The radio host muttered to the young photographer, "Take some pictures of that," which she did.

*"My wife put me in here. I was in here for ten years,"* the old man told Rob.

*"You know what's funny? I outlived that bitch."*

*"The longer you sit there, the spookier it gets."*

After the asylum closed in 1973, the village of Bartonville tried to sell the buildings. It seemed a shame to let the buildings just sit empty. Some of the larger buildings became home to various businesses. But most of the lovely cottages simply sat empty for several years. The cottages weren't big enough for any industrial use. Then again, they were far too big to be cozy little office buildings. Many of the cottages, therefore, fell to the wrecking ball. They were the first of the asylum buildings to be demolished. The buildings were razed, and the debris was simply pushed into the hole where the basement of each cottage had once been. The demolition crews picked up any leftover wreckage in the buckets of bulldozers, and dumped it into the ravines.

The ravines are a souvenir hunter's dream. I had thought that after all this time, there would be very little left down there, but I was wrong, wrong, wrong. You can't walk two paces down in the ravines without stepping on broken crockery. Shards of white porcelain lie everywhere. Sometimes, where the walls of the ravine have been washed away by fall rains, you can see layers of broken dishes four, five, six feet deep, perfect cutaways of dirt and debris. There are broken toilets down there, and pieces of soup tureens, and handleless cups, and thousands of broken dinner plates, all of it the same utilitarian white porcelain, elegant in its spare simplicity. There are chunks of stoneware crocks, used to make sauerkraut. There are fragments of odd, intricate terra cotta work – wall decorations from the razed cottages. There is, incongruously, a cement birdbath sitting upright in the middle of the ravine.

Chris says it's a good idea to have a recorder running as you're poking around the ravines. The spirits get very interested when people go exploring down there. "The longer you sit there, picking through the artifacts, the spookier and spookier it gets," she says.

She and Stacy were exploring one afternoon. Luckily, they took a recorder with them, and left it running as they poked around. Chris said, "Let's walk to the other side." Moments later, a ghostly voice appeared on the recording.

*"Mm-kay."*

Later, another spirit chimed in with an opinion: *"We like the running water."*

*A Paranormal Boundary*

A medium, whom I'll call "Scott", was one of the many people who explored the hilltop as kids. Scott said he's been into every single building at one time or another. He noticed an interesting phenomenon early on in his visits.

He and his friends would cross the ravines to get onto the bluff top. They'd do this – in the dark – by making their way across a large concrete drainage pipe. They realized after a few visits that if their flashlights were on as they crossed the ravine, the lights would fade and die, and no amount of clicking the button or smacking the flashlights on the heel of a hand would get them to work again. But if they crossed the ravine in the dark, then turned the flashlights on once they got onto the asylum grounds, the lights would work perfectly for the rest of the evening.

Scott's theory is that the ravines may represent a "paranormal boundary" around the bluff top. With what we know about running water amplifying the paranormal, this makes sense. Also, the ravines do roughly outline the bluff top.

I had my own odd experience in Cemetery 3 a few summers ago. I went out just to stroll around the cemetery – it was actually my first visit to any of the asylum graveyards. I pulled up to the entrance, the tires of my car crunching on the gravel. I parked and got out. The entrance to the graveyard is marked by a heavy iron chain strung between two solid posts. The chain is there simply to discourage people from driving into the cemetery – there's plenty of room for someone on foot to walk into the graveyard.

It was a bright sunny day in August, the sky a brilliant blue, cloudless except for one tiny snatch of cloud near the sun. As I walked around the right-hand post, that little scrap of cloud moved to cover the sun, and the beautiful day turned overcast.

I wandered around between the headstones, reading numbers and dates. I worked my way all the way down to the edge of the treeline. The gloom continued as I strolled back up through the cemetery. As I passed the chain that marked the entrance, the sun came out from behind that little bit of cloud, and by the time I got into my car, I was reaching for my sunglasses. "That was weird," I muttered as I turned the key in the ignition and backed down the gravel driveway.

Was this another example of a paranormal boundary? It sure felt like it.

The cemeteries at the Peoria State Hospital are the final resting place of over four thousand people. They had their problems in life, as we all do. But when they passed on, each one of them had a respectful funeral. Dr. Zeller and his staff treated these patients like members of one big family. In death, the staff of the hospital showed their patients the consideration they'd have given any beloved family member. Dr. Zeller and Sophie called all the patients "our children". And the ones that had passed on were simply "our sleeping children".

The cemeteries here were intended to be places of quiet, peaceful reflection. After all, many of the people buried here left loved ones behind to mourn them. With the help of Mattie Sutton and other volunteers, the gravesites are slowly being rescued from decades of neglect. Each of the cemeteries is rich in history, and each has its own distinct character. The old soldiers and others sleep in Cemetery 1. The patients in Cemetery 3 repose on either side of their "Glory Walk".

And in Cemetery 2, the descendants of Old Book's Graveyard Elm, mere saplings at the time of his death, now stand watch over his grave and the graves of the other silent dead.

# THE INFLUENCE OF THE PEORIA STATE HOSPITAL

Chris Morris has acquired the reputation of being the "go-to" person when it comes to the history of the Peoria State Hospital. She can usually be found at the Pollak Hospital, and folks in the area know it.

"The tenants on the buildings around here will come over and ask, 'What was here before us?' They want to know what purpose their building served before their business moved in."

Most of the cottages have been torn down, but other buildings were put up in their place. These buildings, too, are home to the spirits that reside on the hilltop.

"Some patients lived here for most of their lives – and with three square meals of healthy, locally-grown food a day, a safe place to live, and interesting things to occupy their time, their lives could last decades. Some of our patients lived here for over fifty years. They felt comfortable here, so it's here they've chosen to return to after death."

*"Out of all the places we went, this was the best one."*

The hilltop also provides perennially interesting fodder for the media every October. WCBU, the local public radio station, has been out to the asylum a couple of times. In 2011, a reporter from the station went on an investigation of the Pollak Hospital with Illinois Ghost Seekers Society. Several years before that, Brian Sieworek, another WCBU reporter, went out to the Bowen Building with Rob Conover as his guide. "Ed" and "Al" were still hanging around the Bowen at that time, so they got a mention on the air. Rob and the reporter were unable to go inside the Bowen at the time, but the spirits appeared to them anyway. "Ed" manifested as a glow of blue ectoplasm, and "Al" glowed white. Brian walked with Rob around the outside of the building in the quiet darkness. At one point, his recorder captured a voice humming three notes, climbing upwards in pitch. Brian was kind enough to share the mp3 with me. I appreciate his generosity, and WCBU's willingness to share that recording with all of you.

I spoke with two reporters from WMBD, Channel 31. The one who worked the camera told me that when they'd been filming a segment for Halloween at the Bowen Building, their camera caught a bright orb floating and dodging lazily around one of the windows.

"There was no wind the day we were filming, no reason for anything to be moving like that. It was weird," he said. "I was watching the footage, and I said, okay, I'm done. That's just too bizarre for me."

Illinois Ghost Seekers Society accompanied Jason Parkinson and "Intern Chad" from Power Peoria 92.3 in an investigation of the Pollak Hospital in October 2011. Their experiences there are documented both on the IGSS website (illinoisghost.com) and on the radio's website (powerpeoria.com – search "Paranormal Peoria" to find the file).

The group started their investigation at the Bowen Building. Excitement was running high, and Jason mentioned on camera that the asylum visit was the most highly anticipated segment of all their "field trips" that the station had planned around Halloween that year.

The group started their investigation at the Bowen Building. The cameraman was filming the introduction for the video that the radio station would later post on YouTube. The Bowen, being so familiar, seemed like the perfect place to start. The group was at the side of the building nearest Constitution Drive (at the door where Trish Weiss has so often seen the White Lady and where the sensitive Merilee Mitchell was prevented from doing her photography by the intensity of the feelings emanating from the side door).

The group ended their recording there too, bringing the short film about the asylum full circle by closing with the Bowen in the background once again. This time, the cameraman, Evan Ford, saw a ghostly figure in one of the windows. "All of a sudden it was there," he said. He snapped a photo and captured the mysterious figure.

The excitement continued as the group explored the Pollak Hospital. The basement, of course, did not disappoint. The radio station reporters were suitably impressed by the creep factor of the morgue. The cameraman caught a shadow zipping past the camera. Chad, the intern, was particularly affected by the chilly temperatures down in the morgue. "This wasn't like a draft or a normal breeze or anything. This goes *through* you." The investigators also heard unexplained footsteps in the main hallway while they were down in the basement.

The reporters from Power Peoria, young guys working for a popular radio station, went into the Pollak with a "prove it" attitude -- "Make us believe." When I spoke with Jason and Chad, about a month after their visit to the Pollak, they seemed satisfied with their experience.

"We didn't go in with high expectations, but what we did get, we felt was worthwhile," Jason told me. "Out of all the places we went that October, that was probably the best one. It wasn't huge, but it was something out of the ordinary."

*Inspiration*

Barry Cloyd is a musician based in the Peoria area. In addition to performing Celtic-inspired music and tunes with an Americana flavor to them, he also writes and performs original material. Easygoing, with an engineer's cap, a salt-and-pepper beard, and a ready grin, he looks the part of a folksy entertainer.

I caught up with Barry after a performance at The Cantina, a bar in downtown Pekin. We chatted for a bit, and he asked me what projects I had in the works. I told him that I was writing a book about the hauntings at the asylum in Bartonville.

"Oh, that's the story about Old Book!"

"That's the one," I said, pleased that he had recognized it.

"Tell me the story again," he encouraged. I told him the tale of Bookbinder, how "Old Book" would weep at every funeral he attended, and how at his own funeral, his ghost was seen at the Graveyard Elm, mourning one last time.

"Wow, that would make a *great* song!"

So maybe, the next time Barry Cloyd performs somewhere, he'll debut "The Ballad of Old Book".


*"I've fallen in love with Dr. George Zeller!"*

While working on this book, I got an email from a filmmaker, a woman named Janette Marie. She invited me to be a part of the documentary she was putting together, a film she was calling *For the Incurable Insane*. I was one of about a dozen people she had lined up to interview. Janette sent me a list of questions, and we set up a time to meet at the asylum.

The day we agreed to meet for filming was cold and *very* windy. (It was November in Illinois. Of course it was cold and windy.) We set up in a somewhat sheltered corner behind the Bowen Building. The wind still caused some noise, buffeting the microphone with blasts of gusty sound. Waiting until the weather was kinder, though, was not an option – since Janette had travelled from LA to make the documentary.

So, we huddled in the dubious protection of the stone walls of the Bowen, and I told Janette stories about the place. I repeated some of the encounters other people had had, and I gave her a quick rundown of the history of the asylum. I emphasized that the asylum was not a place of torture and fear, but of caring and acceptance. As I spoke, I saw Janette nodding behind the camera in silent agreement.

After Janette went back to LA to put the documentary together, I continued to work on this book. At some point, I realized I had to include this chapter, about the far-reaching influence of the Peoria State Hospital. I wrote to Janette, turning the tables, and presented her with a list of questions about her involvement with the asylum.

First of all, I was astounded that she had come all the way to central Illinois from southern California to do a documentary. I learned that Janette grew up in Ottawa, less than two hours north of the asylum.

"Before moving to LA, I used to work as a model, and I often had to travel for gigs." For one session, she had to travel south, to a part of Illinois she had never been before.

"On the way there, I passed this extravagant abandoned building that seemed to dwarf everything else on the whole drive. I made a note of its location, and made sure to visit on my return."

On her trip back, Janette parked near the Bowen, the building that had captured her attention. She wanted to walk around the grounds, to try to figure out what the building had been. (Her guess was a school.) The Bowen itself soon set her straight.

"While exploring, I felt very overwhelmed with a sense of urgency, and an almost unwelcomed feeling. Where I could have spent weeks exploring, after only a few minutes, I quickly became distressed and left immediately. Later that evening, I did some research and discovered the place was an abandoned and haunted insane asylum, which came as a complete surprise to me."

Later, she moved to California and started on a career in film. When it came time to tackle her first short documentary, she racked her brains trying to think of a project she could research and complete in only a few months. "I remembered back to three years previous when I had stumbled upon that amazing abandoned building. I realized I had forgotten all about the place, and instantly I had to learn more."

I asked her if she was mainly interested in the asylum's history, or if the paranormal aspect of the site intrigued her. Her answer mirrored my feelings exactly.

"When I first learned of the asylum, I found both aspects completely fascinating. What came as the biggest surprise to me was that the Peoria State Hospital had a brighter past than most mental asylums around the world." Janette has incorporated this into her documentary. The list of people she interviewed for the film included not only paranormal experts, but historians too. She made sure to include people who would help her tell the entirely compelling story of the Peoria State Hospital, its compassionate past as well as its haunted present.

"This project has become a world of importance to me – not only the film itself, but also the stories compiled within the film. These are the real stories of real people who never had the chance to tell their story. It's been a really emotional journey."

Janette chuckled. "I have to laugh because it really is hilarious … I've fallen in love with Dr. George Zeller, who died in 1938. I'm seriously considering getting this fantastic portrait of him tattooed on my arm. What an amazing man he was."

The preview of *For the Incurable Insane* has been released, and can be seen on YouTube.

*Reality's End Films*

Brandon Lamprecht and his friends started off doing comedy sketches on YouTube. Making people laugh was great, but the three guys soon decided that they also wanted to make people think. They wanted to do something more serious. The friends had heard about the asylum, so they contacted Chris Morris to brainstorm ideas for a film.

"Chris suggested we do a film about Old Book," Brandon told me. "That project started out with one of the craziest experiences we've ever had."

The group went out to Cemetery 2 very late at night, around eleven o'clock. "We'd sort of had this idea that no one knew where Old Book's gravestone was, that it would be really hard to find. Well, I literally tripped over it. I've still got a scar on my ankle from falling over Bookbinder's headstone."

Of course, being filmmakers, the guys had a camera running as they wandered through the cemetery looking for Bookbinder's grave. After Brandon stumbled over the headstone, his friend took some footage of the grave.

"As we filmed the headstone, this weird shadow showed up on the stone," Brandon said. "It looked like the profile of a person – you could see ears and a nose. It wasn't either one of us; we made sure of where we were standing when we were filming."

Brandon and his friends worked up a script and shot the film. Brandon told me, with no small amount of pride, that they were the last filmmakers to be allowed to go into the Bowen before it was closed for several years due to the asbestos inside. "We shot the last 'legal' footage of the interior," he boasted.

*The Asylum Chronicles I: Bookbinder* is an excellent look at the tale of Old Book. It's a period piece, told as a reminiscence by Dr. Zeller. As it is made for entertainment, rather than as a documentary, the writers took some poetic license with the film, but that only adds to the powerful storytelling.

"The first night we showed the film, on the grounds of the Bowen, two hundred people showed up to watch a seventeen-minute movie. The next weekend, we showed it at Landmark Theatre. The one theater sold out, and they had to open another one." The Bookbinder film has been aired on fifty-seven different public access channels in Illinois, from the Chicago suburbs to Springfield. You can find it on YouTube.

Reality's End Films is currently working on another project involving the Peoria State Hospital. The company made a short film about Rhoda Derry, and is also working on a full-length film about her. The short clip, as well as the five-minute demo for the full-length movie, is available on the Internet.

Again, the writers took poetic liberties with the story of Rhoda Derry. There are many details of her life before she was committed to the Adams County almshouse that we simply don't know, details that are lost forever. But in imagining Rhoda's life, and her relationship with her beau, the filmmakers bring her tragic story to brilliant life.

The movie itself will be part documentary, part feature film. Brandon and the other people involved with the project made the decision to tell Rhoda's story both ways, presenting the fact as a documentary, with actors interpreting the characters in the drama. Even with guessing at some of the story, this film of Rhoda Derry's life is a powerful piece of work. Even the five-minute teaser, set to the music of U2's "With or Without You", captures the harrowing agony of lost love. The full-length film, currently in production, will be well worth the wait.

# A FEW FINAL THOUGHTS

I am, fortunately or unfortunately (depending on how you look at it), uniquely qualified to write a book on a haunted asylum. In addition to living just a short car or motorcycle ride away from Bartonville, and in addition to being a paranormal investigator already, I come from a long line of crazies. Several of them even have the paperwork to prove it. A great-uncle and a cousin have committed suicide, the great-uncle by drinking muriatic acid. My great-grandmother, a frustrated poet, took to writing rambling, semi-legible notes on anything that would hold still long enough, including her desk, any cardboard box that happened to be sitting around, and the handle of her favorite rake. We still have a jewelry box, a souvenir from the Brookfield Zoo, on which she had made her own mark: "Polar bears have cool fun at the zoo." She signed everything "MYZ" (her initials), and the date. I suppose it was her way of showing ownership of virtually everything she touched. She also had a full-blown phobia about the mail. When I was a small child, I'd run to the mailbox when I visited, and bring the mail that was hers up to her room. She'd make me go wash my hands immediately, saying that letters were filthy things. My grandfather (her son) was a recovering alcoholic who required that his wife dry each of his ice cubes with a towel before putting them in his drink, so they wouldn't stick together in the glass. There is no shortage of random weirdness in my family tree, behavior that in another time would most likely have gotten any one of us tossed into the bughouse. We have issues ranging from mild depression to gender dysphoria and narcissistic personality disorder, from anger management issues and vicious migraines to crossdressing and dumpster diving.

My mother tried several times to commit suicide. She suffered from some sort of schizoaffective disorder; not schizophrenia exactly, but multiple personalities. Quite simply, she didn't know who she was most of the time. Some of her journal entries are simply a laundry list of medications, others the ramblings of a tortured mind. But the few moments of lucidity reveal glimpses of a brilliant, acerbic wit – something my sister and I have both inherited from her. These are tantalizing hints of the woman she could have been, if her brain had simply been wired differently. It was a tremendous effort to be her; it was a victory for her if she was able to get out of bed and dressed by four o'clock in the afternoon, let alone care for two small children. She spent most of her life in a haze of prescription drugs and delusions, wondering just who it was she was supposed to be. She finally died by accident, when I was five years old and my sister was two, as a direct result of all those meds. It was a few days after New Year's 1975. She took her prescription-strength sleeping pills, then went to take the garbage out. She slipped on the icy back steps and hit her head, but was too groggy from the pills to get up. So she just lay there on the ice and went to sleep.

As I was writing this book, my mom (my father's second wife) was admitted to the hospital with heart problems. Her defibrillator had gone off because she had suffered a manic break, and a few days later, she signed herself into the psych ward at the hospital as a voluntary committal. My sister, one of her caregivers, says that this private hospital beat the heck out of the state institution where Mom spent some time twenty years ago. Some things never change, and money still makes things go a lot smoother.

I myself have struggled with depression, along with millions of other Americans. It's not an exclusive club. I know from bitter experience how much depression hurts. I know the terror that comes in the night, when your brain just won't work the way it's supposed to, when the things that used to bring you pleasure and satisfaction just seem gray and hollow and worthless. I *know*. And I know there's a history of mental illness in my family. Any crossed wires or misfiring connections I've got upstairs, I come by them honestly.

But all this, all the personal and hereditary bats in my attic, it's all given me a unique perspective from which to examine the hauntings at the Peoria State Hospital. To me, these spirits aren't just lost souls. I understand, more than most, the pain that these people went through. I have a lot of sympathy for the people these ghosts used to be. And I have made it my business, over the past few months, to try to communicate with them, as far as I am able.

I've said it before: I'm not a medium, and I'm not especially sensitive. I'm about as receptive as a dining room table. I have no way of sensing the Other Side, except for what my instruments pick up, or when someone really wants to get close to me, the way "Christopher" did.

So why do I do it? Why do I keep going out to the ruins of the asylum, time after time, asking my questions of the empty air, hoping that this time I'll get a response? Why do I spend hours taping, and hours more listening to those recordings, in the hope of catching some little snippet of sound that my brain can interpret as words from the beyond? Why do I stay out way too late, poking around in the dark, seeking evidence? Why do I get so excited to hear a blurt of sound from a ghost box, and why do I accept the pitying smiles of the skeptics when I share my findings with people who don't believe in the afterlife with that same passion that I do?

There's the flippant answer: why not? Everyone needs a hobby. But I think the answer can and should go deeper than that.

Here's what all serious paranormal investigators instinctively know – it truly is okay to talk "to the air". You *need* to do it. The deceased need to hear you, too. If you want to look at it another way, it's basic scientific law – energy is neither created nor destroyed. It's the First Law of Thermodynamics, and you don't have to be a physics wonk to grasp it. It's just neat, that's all, that science backs up the idea that death does not kill the vital essence of who we are.

Thousands of people lived at the Peoria State Hospital. Some of them recovered and went on to lead happy, productive lives. Some of them died here. There are over four thousand graves in the cemeteries around the grounds. Even so, fewer than half of the people who died at the asylum were buried here. The rest were claimed by their relatives and buried elsewhere, in family plots. There were a lot of deaths here on this hill. There are a lot of spirits that remain here.

A few of these spirits still wander the remaining buildings steeped in a sense of fear and dread, or petulant anger. But most of them seem to have found acceptance, and a measure of peace. The Peoria State Hospital was a unique institution in the history of mental health care. Under Dr. Zeller's supervision, it became a model for state hospitals everywhere. Dr. Zeller himself revolutionized the treatment of mental illness. He went out of his way to rescue the most severe, most pathetic cases from the squalor and terror of the almshouses, and he brought them to his hospital. There, they were cared for and their illnesses were treated. Perhaps most importantly, they were separated according to their affliction. They were finally – maybe for the first time in their lives – among others that were going through the same experiences they were, who understood exactly the misery they endured. This had to have been an incredible relief to these patients. No wonder they thought of the asylum as home. The word "asylum" means a place of refuge, a place of respite and rest, a place to go to be safe.

And maybe it's not just the patients that walk these halls when the sun goes down. We've heard stories of nurses who died at the hospital, and we've examined evidence that seems to point to some of them staying on after death. Maybe the spirits of those dedicated professionals – maybe even the spirit of Dr. Zeller himself – help to infuse these buildings with feelings of caring and peace.

There is something undeniable about this site, some strange, powerful draw to it even in its decrepit state. People are devoted to these grounds, and fight like hell to save the remaining buildings and to preserve the cemeteries. I've met scores of these fans, and at times, their passion can become nearly rabid. What is it about the Peoria State Hospital that inspires such rapt attention?

Part of it, I think, lies with the spirit of Dr. George A. Zeller. His pioneering techniques inspired devotion in both his staff and in his patients. He was beloved by the population of the hospital, and in return, he dedicated his life to easing the misery of the mentally ill. That takes guts. Mental illness has few outward physical signs. A nurse at the Zeller Mental Health Center put it especially well: "It's very hard to keep reminding yourself that these people are very ill when you don't see any blood. You don't see the fever inside of them." The mentally ill, or mentally disabled, often act weirdly, or even turn violent. It's not an easy thing, to care for people suffering like this. It's stressful, and to this day there's still a powerful taboo attached to mental illness. Dr. Zeller's importance to the field of mental health care can't be overstated.

Dr. Zeller pioneered other fields as well. He insisted that his female attendants be as well-trained in patient care – even care of violent patients – as male attendants. He developed a first-class nursing program at the institution. He felt that the soft touch and kind words of a woman were a balm to the troubled mind of someone suffering from insanity. In short, he advanced the cause of "women's lib" years before the rest of the country caught up to him. Dr. Zeller respected women, and that respect came through in all his dealings with his staff. They in turn adored him for it.

The Peoria State Hospital was so radically different from most other institutions during its years of operation that it only makes sense that its afterlife is different too. People ask, "Well, if there wasn't any abuse, why is the asylum so haunted?" The answer is simple: this was home. Zeller and his staff strove to make this institution as much like a private home as possible. The cottage system, with a married couple in charge of each cottage, helped foster that needed illusion.

Ghosts can be bound to a place by fear. That's absolutely true. But ghosts can also be drawn back to a place by feelings of love and caring. If a place felt like home in life, an earthbound spirit will be drawn back to it after death. It's the difference between a tortured spirit being bound to a place, and a ghost returning by choice to a place where it knew peace and contentment during life.

I honestly thought that I would have more trouble than I did, in researching this book. I assumed that the businesses around the Bowen Building would be hesitant to share any information with me. I figured the owners would want to avoid any association with an asylum, especially one that was reputedly haunted.

There are a few business owners that do feel this way. (So I wasn't completely wrong about that.) But most of the people I talked to were eager to share their stories. And it wasn't only in Bartonville that this happened. The asylum's reputation reached well across the river, into Pekin and East Peoria. People wanted to share their memories of the asylum, as well as their ghost stories. For the most part, these stories weren't whispered tales told out of school. I didn't personally hear any stories of abuse – not a one. Most of the memories people shared with me were pleasantly nostalgic, their recollections of visiting loved ones who happened to be going through some mental or emotional difficulties that meant a stay at the Peoria State Hospital.

The people that did have ghost stories to tell shared them with equal gusto. In Bartonville, it doesn't have to be October for people to get into a good ghost story.

And the people who volunteer at the remaining asylum buildings, the Bowen and the Pollak, are absolutely passionate about them and the history they represent. These two buildings haven't been transmogrified into businesses. They are the representations of the asylum as it once was, and of what it was, sadly, allowed to become. The Pollak Hospital is kept as much in its original state as possible, to help visitors imagine what it was like when it functioned as a tuberculosis ward. The volunteers at the Pollak are passionate in their dedication to interpreting its history. The Bowen Building is the grand old lady of the hilltop, but its present state of decay mirrors the decline of the asylum in its later years of operation. Fortunately, though, the Bowen has a group of eager volunteers who spend hours cleaning up the place, both on the grounds and now, inside the building.

I've met lots of ghost hunters over the course of writing this book. They seem to be split about equally between male and female. But it is the women that are most vocal about their passion for the Peoria State Hospital. Chris Morris speaks of the hospital as if it's still open, as if she is a part of it, as if it's a living, breathing entity – "We had movies every weekend, we made our own clothes, we were the first to institute an eight-hour workday." Janette Marie, the filmmaker, admits to having fallen in love with Dr. Zeller. She's even thinking of getting his portrait tattooed on her arm.

I have to confess that I've fallen under the spell of the place myself. If I had to choose only one haunted site to investigate for the rest of my life, I would happily stick with the hospital and its grounds. I suppose you could say that this asylum, its history and its personalities, have ruined me for all other haunted sites.

In all seriousness, though, I do think that the spirit of Dr. Zeller – not necessarily his ghost, but the spirit of responsibility and caring with which he imbued this hospital during his tenure – is the magnetism that draws people, especially women, to this site. Dr. Zeller had such a strong will to do good and to care for the less fortunate, it's no wonder his spirit chooses to wander this bluff top. Once you've been here a few times, whether you've wandered around outside the Bowen, poked through the Pollak, or simply strolled through the cemeteries, there's a strange pull to the place. The whole hilltop just seems to get under your skin. No one seems to be able to explain it; they just accept it.

I've been lucky enough to meet many of the people that have fallen under the spell of the Peoria State Hospital. Now, in these pages, you've met them too. I hope that if you're ever in the Peoria area, you make the time to visit the grounds of the asylum. Walk through the cemeteries, and give a passing thought to those who sleep beneath that grass. Have a drink at Stone Country, and see if you can hear the faint ghostly thump of basketballs on the polished floor. Gaze up at the blank windows of the Bowen Building.

Someone may be looking back at you.

# BIBLIOGRAPHY

*Asylum: Inside the Closed World of State Mental Hospitals.* Payne, Christopher, with an essay by Oliver Sacks, c 2009 Massachusetts Institute of Technology

*Asylum Light: Stories From the Dr. George A. Zeller Era and Beyond; Peoria State Hospital, Galesburg Mental Health Center, and George A. Zeller Mental Health Center.* Ward, James Sheridan et al, with memories collected by Arlene Parr, c 2004 Mental Health Historic Preservation Society of Central Illinois

*Bittersweet Memories: A History of the Peoria State Hospital.* Lisman, Gary, with memories collected by Arlene Parr, c 2005 Trafford Publishing

*Illinois Public Mental Health Services: 1847 to 2000.* Mehr, Joseph J., PhD, c 2002 Trafford Publishing

*The Lives They Left Behind: Suitcases From a State Hospital Attic.* Penney, Darby and Peter Stastny, c 2008 Bellevue Literary Press

*The Lobotomist: A Maverick Medical Genius and His Tragic Quest to Rid the World of Mental Illness.* El-Hai, Jack, c 2005 John Wiley and Sons

*Logan County Insanity Record, 1856 – 1963, An Index and Synopsis,* compiled by Sylvia Zethmayr, Illinois Regional Archives Depository, c 1992

*Madness: An American History of Mental Illness and Its Treatment.* deYoung, Mary, c 2010 McFarland & Company

*Mary, Me: In Search of a Lost Lifetime.* Baker, Rick, c 1989 The Bakery

*Women of the Asylum: Voices From Beyond the Walls, 1840 – 1945.* Geller, Jeffrey L. and Maxine Harris, c 1994 Doubleday

# APPENDIX

*Illinois Paranormal Research Groups*

*(Arranged by year of founding)*

*Reprinted with gracious permission from Haunting Illinois: A Tourist's Guide to the Weird & Wild Places of the Prairie State, 2nd Edition by Michael Kleen (Second Edition c 2011 Thunder Bay Press)*

1977

Ghost Trackers Club/Ghost Research Society

www.ghostresearch.org


1992

Midwest Paranormal Society

www.hauntedmidwest.org


1996

American Ghost Society

www.prairieghosts.com/ags.html

Central Illinois Investigative Team

www.myspace.com/cipiteam

1998

Haunted Chicagoland/Joliet Paranormal Society

www.jolietparanormal.com

The Fallen

www.trueillinoishaunts.com/the-fallen/

1999

Illinois Paranormal Society

www.illinoisparanormalsociety.webs.com

2001

Crawford County Ghost Hunters

www.crawfordcountyghosthunters.com

2002

Christian County Ghost Hunters Society

www.parastudies.ning.com

(TIPS) Tazewell Illinois Paranormal Society

www.tazewellparanormal.com

2004

(SciFi Channel's *Ghost Hunters* premiered on October 6, 2004)

Southern Illinois Ghost Hunting Team

www.sight1.tk

Will County Ghost Hunters Society

www.aghostpage.com

2005

Northern Illinois Paranormal Investigation Society

www.nipis.org

Shelby Paranormal Research Society

www.myspace.com/shelbyparanormalsociety

2006

Chicago Paranormal Research Society

www.chicagoparanormal.org

Confidential Paranormal Investigators

www.cpiteam.net

Illinois Ghost Hunters

www.illinoisghosthunters.com

Paranormal Anomaly Search Team

www.pastinvestigators.com

Paranormal Moms Society

www.paranormalmomssociety.com

Springfield Paranormal Research Group

www.springfieldparanormal.info


2007

DuPage Paranormal Society

www.dupageparanormal.com

Elgin Paranormal Investigators

www.elginparanormalinvestigators.com

Ghost and Paranormal Society

www.theghostandparanormalsociety.yolasite.com

Illinois Paranormal Society

www.myspace.com/illinoisparanormalsc

Insight Dimension Paranormal Research Group

www.nitey-niteghosttours.com

Little Egypt Ghost Society

Mid America Ghost Hunters

www.magh.biz

New Age Paranormal

www.newageparanormal.com

Southern Illinois Ghost Hunting Society

www.sigh-il.tripod.com

2008

Central Illinois Paranormal Investigators

www.cipi.us.com

Dekalb County Paranormal Society

Dupage Researchers and Investigators of the Paranormal

www.driparanormal.com

GUARD (Ghost Unit Analysis Research Detection)

(Google "GUARD Paranormal")

Midwest Haunting

www.myspace.com/hauntedmacomb

Paranormal Research of Illinois

www.paranormal-research-of-illinois.com

Prairieland Paranormal Society

www.myspace.com/prairielandparanormal

River Town Paranormal Society

www.RiverTownParanormalSociety.net

Rockford Interdisciplinary Para-Investigations

www.facebook.com/RockfordRIP

Windy City Paranormal

www.windycityparanormal.com


2009

Central Illinois Ghost Hunters

www.centralillinoisghosthunters.com

Forest City Paranormal Society

www.forest-city-paranormal-society.com

RIP (Research in Paranormal)

www.ripillinois.org

Rural Illinois Paranormal Society

SPIRIT (Shane's Paranormal Investigative Research Intelligence Team)

www.spiritghosthunting.com

Wabash Area Paranormal Society

www.wabashghosthunters.com


2010

Illinois Ghost Seekers Society

www.illinoisghost.com

River to River Paranormal Group

# ≈ACKNOWLEDGMENTS

This book quite literally could not have been written without the help of many, many, *many* people. I'd like to thank them all here.

Firstly, a huge thanks to all of those wonderful volunteers at both the Bowen Building and the Pollak Hospital. It's thanks to all of you that I have these great, spooky stories. Thank you all so much for being so generous with your time, your knowledge of the Peoria State Hospital, and your tales.

Thanks to the authors who came before me, especially Gary Lisman and James Sheridan Ward. You're part of the reason I wrote this book. Special thanks to Arlene Parr, the project director for the Mental Health Historic Preservation Society of central Illinois.

A *huge* thank you to all the people who shared their stories with me for this book. I hope you get a kick out of seeing your name in print. If I have missed anyone, or left out any fun stories, the fault is all mine.

Thank you to Dr. George Zeller, whose vision resulted in there being an abandoned asylum for us all to explore. It may seem like I'm being facetious, and I apologize for that. I'd like to thank Dr. Zeller for his compassion and his dedication to the mentally ill of Illinois and of the world. Because of his work, and the work of his staff, Bartonville is home not only to a haunted asylum, but to a legacy of caring that goes far beyond a simple bughouse. I'm really proud to live just across the river from a place like that.

To the members of the Dark Continents Publishing family, thank you all so very much. It's so good to know that we're all in this together, and that we've all got each other's backs. David, Tracie, Ade, you guys are awesome. And Donnie, thanks loads for the fabulous cover art you always work up for me. You're the best!

The biggest thank you of all goes to my husband, Rob. Thank you for understanding this weird obsession of mine. Thank you for cutting me slack when I stay out until three in the morning hunting ghosts. And thank you for always being there for me. Love you, babe.

# ABOUT THE AUTHOR

Sylvia Shults started her career in paranormal investigation with her first nonfiction book, *Ghosts of the Illinois River*. The research quickly grew into an obsession, cementing her childhood fascination with ghost stories. How cool is it to find out that ghost stories can be true? Shults is also the author of many fiction books, writing both horror and romance. Her books include the horror short story collection *The Dark at the Heart of the Diamond* and the humorous romance *Double Double Love & Trouble* (both Dark Continents Publishing). She works at a library in Illinois, the better to feed her reading addiction. She lives with her husband, a furry German Shepherd daughter, and three obnoxious cats. She loves hearing from readers, so please visit her on the Web at sylviashults.com or on any of her Facebook fan pages (Darkheart for horror, Sparkleheart for romance, or Ghosts of the Illinois River or Fractured Spirits for ghost stuff).

*MEDIA ENHANCED BOOK*

*Dark Continents provides more, to make this book come alive!*

Oh, don't close the book yet! There's much more to be found on the Internet. For more information, please visit the Fractured Spirits fan page on Facebook. The QR code below will take you right there. That's where you'll find recordings of the EVPs you've just read about, along with links to videos, and more photographs. You'll also find announcements of investigations and other cool things happening at the Peoria State Hospital, and places where I'll be doing lectures or signings of the book. And remember, that page is there for you. If you go exploring at the Peoria State Hospital, and you run into a ghost or two, we want to hear about it! Go to the fan page and tell us about it. Enjoy your visit!

*Audio – listen to EVPs and other audio files*

*Video – watch video clips from ghost investigations*

*Pictures – see photos taken by ghost hunters*

*Discussion – post your own experiences at the Peoria State Hospital!*

CPSIA information can be obtained
at www.ICGtesting.com
Printed in the USA
BVOW10s1945080217
475635BV00002B/133/P